THE MIRACULOUS REALM OF HEAVEN ON EARTH

LIVING LIFE ON THE OTHER SIDE
OF RESURRECTION

HILA J. ESTERS

AUTHOR ACADEMY elite

Also by Hila J. Esters

DADDY'S LITTLE GIRL

YOUR DADDY'S SO-O-O BIG …

Published by Author Academy Elite
PO Box 43, Powell, OH 53035
www.AuthorAcademyElite.com

Library of Congress Control Number: 2020903841

Paperback: 978-1-64746-173-7
Hardback: 978-1-64746-174-4
E-book: 978-1-64746-175-1

Available in paperback, hardback, e-book, and audiobook

All notes from scriptures are taken from the King James Bible which is public domain.

The book referenced is offered as a resource. It is not intended in any way to be or imply an endorsement by Author Academy Elite, nor does Author Academy Elite vouch for the content of the material for the life of this book.

DEDICATION

I dedicate The Miraculous Realm of Heaven on Earth to my mother. Because she dreamed of a better life for her family, against enormous odds, she made and followed through on a series of difficult decisions. Her boldness and specific actions provided us with better opportunities that changed our lives.

I also dedicate this book to all of you who refuse to settle for the dictates of life. Thinking that what you are experiencing is all there is to living stifles your ability to progress. Decide to step out of the rank and file of the crowd. Look up and out, expecting to see more. You will. What you see and act on will change your life.

CONTENTS

PART 4: STRATEGIC PREPARATION – POSITION

PART 5: THE KINGDOM LIFESTYLE – PREEMINENCE

A NOTE TO THE READER

The Miraculous Realm of Heaven on Earth can be read and applied personally or used for group study as follows:

- Read the book chapter by chapter.

- Read each chapter, then in the section immediately following the current chapter, answer the study questions.

- Read each chapter, then in the section immediately following the current chapter, answer the study questions, and then study the scriptures from the references given.

The scripture references are from the King James Bible. Each reference includes a brief description of the scripture that relates to the chapter text. *The description is **NOT** the actual scripture*. By searching each scripture reference and other scriptures associated with the given scripture reference, you allow the Holy Spirit, who knows the deep things of God, to guide you into a more in-depth personal or group study of the material.

INTRODUCTION

One Answer Changed My Life Forever

Sometimes I wonder what my life would be like if I had not decided, at the age of three, to ask my mother about something that had me puzzled. Every Sunday morning in church service, I spent an hour and a half of my life sitting on hard wooden benches with my parents, my oldest brother, and the twins. The choir sang, the ushers passed a big gold plate to collect the offering, and then the pastor talked a lot about God. Through it all, without success, I tried very hard to sit still. Without fail, boredom would creep up and come me over. One Sunday morning, to entertain myself, I scanned the scenes in the stained glass windows around the sanctuary. I saw Jesus teaching the disciples, his mother Mary, holding him when he was a baby and some sheep. The pastor preached about how good God was, but I couldn't find God anywhere in the stained glass windows. Trying to put together what I listened to each week with what I saw in the windows, didn't make sense to me.

Nowadays, I see children run-up to their parents and interrupt them at will in the middle of their conversations. When I was a child, children didn't interrupt their parents, let alone ask them unnecessary questions. My mother believed in no-nonsense concerning her children. I was three years old. The twins, a boy, and a girl were four years old, and my oldest brother was six. My mother was busy all the time. One Monday morning, following another confusing Sunday message about God, I decided that I had to gain enough courage to interrupt my mother. With the question continuing to bug me in my mind, I had to ask her. Mama was sitting in the dining room, folding clothes. My favorite show was on television in the living room, but my question was more important than cartoons!

Turning to look at Mama, I took a deep breath and stood up. I slowly walked into the dining room, where she was sitting and waited for her to ask me what I wanted. I said, 'Mama, can I ask you a question?' To my relief, she said, 'Yes.' I had thought about the question for so long; it just fell out of my mouth. I said, 'The pastor keeps talking about God, but I can't find him in the stained glass windows. Mama, where's God?' She said, 'God is in heaven. He's invisible, and you can talk to him any time you want.'

God is invisible!' I thought. 'No wonder I couldn't find him!' With relief and excitement, I asked her if I could go outside. To my surprise, she said, 'Yes.' Out in the back yard, I looked for something to sit on. Choosing a spot, I sat down and looked up to the sky. I figured heaven had to be up there somewhere. Then, I wondered, 'What do you say to God?' After thinking about it, I thought the best thing to do was to say hello. I said, 'Hello God, how are you?' Immediately, I heard the words, 'The flowers are beautiful today, aren't they?' In shock, I looked behind me, to the right and the left. No one was there! I turned back around. Staring at the ground, I said to myself, 'God just talked to me! Out loud!'

Suddenly I had a big secret! Who could I tell? Would my brothers and sister believe me? Would Mama think I was lying? Believe me; she had rules about lying. I decided to keep this secret to myself. From that day forward, I tried to find people who would even mention speaking directly to God. To my surprise, no one at my church ever said they did. It wasn't until I was much older and had attended several other churches that I found people who had similar experiences with the Holy Spirit. Despite this, I've continued to develop and enjoy conversations with God. Because of my close relationship with the Holy Spirit, he has taught and guided me throughout my life. I've experienced continual manifestations of the power of God. He uses me to bless others through the Holy Spirit's revelations, prophetic insights, and healing power.

Our mother always told us that no matter what happens, trust God. No matter what has happened in my life, good or bad, he has always been there to help me. God bless my Mama! One answer changed my life forever!

The Miraculous Realm of Heaven on Earth presents spiritual awareness in life with the knowledge and authority to choose upward mobility in the spiritual and natural realms. Suddenly becoming aware that you have been walking through life controlled by outside forces, is an eye-opener. God desires that you experience the goodness of heaven while living here on the earth. Once you discover that real freedom is an option, allow yourself to look at life through a two-way open-ended lens. View the limitless possibilities of living life in the heavenly realm, then turn to scan a panoramic view of humanity's limitations of earthly living.

Become aware of what God and his Son, Jesus Christ have made available to you. Decide to separate yourself from what others call normal. Freedom of movement requires a plan plus personal preparation via the Holy Spirit. Learn to recognize problems and overcome obstacles. Release God's miraculous kingdom, power, and glory from his heart perspective. Pursuing God's way of doing things will transform your life and usher you into living life on the other side of the resurrection of the Lord Jesus Christ, now.

One of the ways God communicates with me is through visions. Most of them have been given early in the morning. One such morning, he showed me an image of a puppet. From this experience, he has given me five steps that will change any situation in your life. I share them in the pages of this book. Plan to progress, change your life, and leave a legacy of life-changing power for others.

PART 1: THE DECISION

Awareness

CHAPTER 1

Are Your Decision-Making Abilities Hampered?

Cut the Strings of Adversity?

Awareness opens the door to the possibility of what was previously unknown. People who are empowered and awakened to their God-given potential can make decisions and follow them through to completion. In contrast, the decision-making abilities of people who live in status-quo, have limiting beliefs, and feed negative emotions remain hampered. Once you become aware that a situation or fact has held you back or locked you down from advancing, various choices begin to present themselves. Thinking, *I can't escape from any area of personal or social growth* hampers your ability to make a well-informed decision.

Early one morning, I awoke to a brief three-part vision. Standing there, held up by dirty old strings, was a filthy, water-stained wooden boy puppet. In the silence of the image, with his head bowed low, and his thin arms hung down at his sides, he stood very still. I couldn't see his eyes, but I knew they were tightly closed. Somehow, I could sense his sadness and pain.

The young boy wore an old-time Swedish hat. A bent, worn-out feather stuck out of the hatband. Tucked in his torn blue cuffed shorts was a painted-on short-sleeved white shirt. Green, tattered suspenders buttoned his shorts. On his feet were scuffed up, dark brown, wooden clog shoes.

Suddenly, without a pull on the strings, he lifted his head. His eyes opened wide as if in shock. Instantly, he had realized something that could no longer remain hidden from him. I stared at the boy intently as the shock of realization slowly dissipated from his eyes. Then gradually, they transformed into a fixed, unshakable determination. For a brief moment, I thought he could see me. I was in shock!

As I continued to watch him, still wondering how he could all of a sudden come alive, his eyes narrowed. The dirty old strings that held him; the tattered, filthy, clothes he wore, and the pain he had suffered no longer mattered. Without help or permission, he quickly lifted his right arm high above his head. In his hand, held perpendicular to the strings, was a large pair of black-handled metal scissors. Without a second thought, he cut the strings! Did he fall? No! He stood there looking at me intently. Wide-eyed, I stared back at him. What he suddenly realized was that he could stand on his own without someone else thinking for him and especially without the manipulation of strings.

Later, as I reflected on the vision, I began to realize that the young puppet represented most of us in various areas of our lives. The unaware, immature puppet represented the manipulation and control by people who lead others to believe that they are in the know. They cunningly take advantage of people who aren't aware of and therefore have no knowledge of the things they don't even realize exist. These people pull the strings of others to advantage themselves.

Let's look at the actions of the manipulated puppet. How and why were the activities of the puppet managed? The puppet master possessed the ability to maneuver each movement of the helpless puppet skillfully. The boy could not see, hear, think, speak, move, or do anything for himself. His appearance and even the painted on clothes he wore were demeaning. In his depressed, helpless state, he could do nothing about the deep sadness and excruciating emotional pain he always endured. In this mental and physically controlled state, he closed his eyes and hung his head. Without knowing the source or reason for the state he was in, how would his life ever change?

Change in your life begins by changing your thinking. Taking the time to investigate how you think about a matter will lead you to why you think about it in that particular way. If you close your eyes, you can open them. If you shut your ears to an idea you have decided not to hear, you can open them again. Inner vision is formed by what you choose to see and hear. How you think makes a choice, and creates the image for you. When you have allowed the words and ideas of others to use your limited views against you, they can use the power you have given them to their advantage. Because they have the freedom of time and vision, they can plan and maneuver every move you make. Using your refusal or unknown lack of ability to hear and see, they have added your limited power to their power. Then when you speak or act, you are actually expressing their thoughts.

Living in an adverse environment of oppression and hopelessness caused by the hidden manipulation of controlled awareness blinds you to your ability to make informed decisions. What you thought to be freedom, was only limited knowledge with calculated movements. To stand on your own, unshakable determination is necessary to break free from those who seek to control you. To even hope to gain the freedom, courage, and confidence needed to make your own decisions, you must have more knowledge and understanding of how to move forward and why.

You desire a better life. You know if given a chance, you can improve yourself and change your life. The problem, you can't figure out, no matter how hard you try, why your circumstances remain the same. Living in this adverse environment of status-quo with limiting beliefs, causes you to feed your negative emotions with a stream of negative thoughts. Thoughts create. Negative thinking produces negative results. Continuously repeating this pattern of negativity hinders you by adding to the problem and not effecting or solving the undesired situation.

Your thoughts create, but God's thoughts create powerful, lasting results. The plans he directs toward you are for your good. They are intended to free you and prosper you by leading you to the conclusion he expects. To obtain the freedom to think, speak, and act on your own, you must hear the truth in a manner that allows you to see it and then be able to relate to it. If you choose to believe and receive the words given, you will continue to receive his direction. Understanding the solution to your problem provides you with a plan, and the courage to take corrective action. Without warning, the puppet lifted his head. His eyes popped wide open with the realization of freedom. Where did the knowledge come from, and how was he able to receive it in his present state?

Powerfully delivered and convincing, the revealed knowledge was far beyond the understanding of the one who manipulated the strings. God had revealed himself to the young puppet, and the boy believed him. All he had to do was follow the instructions. Falling or failing was not an option for him. Convinced of God's power, the puppet received life, lifted his head and opened his eyes. With focused determination, he gathered the courage to take action. Quickly, he raised the scissors over his head, positioned them perpendicular to the strings, and cut them.

No power on earth could hold him down any longer. With fierce tenacity, he stood on his own without someone else thinking for him and manipulating his every move. He was finally free. With no strings attached, the door of opportunity opened. The chance to discover and explore the possibilities of what was previously unknown to him began with valuable information, and one decision to take action.

The vision of the puppet tells you why you need to transition from an unperceived controlled state to where you can receive God's wisdom and knowledge. To break free from the control of others, you must develop the courage to make a firm decision. Before you can discover all the enjoyable possibilities living life holds for you, accepting the fact that God created and formed you for a purpose is just the beginning. In doing so, he filled you with his ability. Knowing this also reveals a valuable key to how you learn from him. Increasing his knowledge in you is the potential you develop, which gives you the courage and power to dominate in every area of your life. His knowledge is power.

No matter what situation you find yourself in, there is always room for improvement with an opportunity for upward mobility in anything you decide to do in life. Why should you bother to consider what God has to offer you rather than depend on yourself or other people? Plenty of self-help professionals, well-meaning family, friends, teachers, and others who suggest their services, books, videos or meetings, etc. are more than willing to help you. Seeking help from God is best because receiving help from others does not necessarily change you on the inside. What do I mean by this? God knows where you are. He knows the thoughts and condition of your heart. Therefore, he knows what you need to advance in life.

Who is God, and where does he dwell? The following is a description from a few bible verses of who God is, where he is, and how, if allowed, he changes your life. You can decide for yourself if allowing him to protect and lead you will result in a better life than what you have been experiencing. God is love and light. He is an eternal, life-giving, immortal Spirit, whose name is Holy. Clothed with honor and majesty, he inhabits eternity. Strength and beauty are in his sanctuary.

God is all-powerful, all-knowing, and he is present everywhere. No matter where you are or where you go, God is there. There is no power higher than him. In the beginning, he created the heaven and the earth. Heaven is his throne, and the earth is his footstool. His kingdom rules and reigns over all other kingdoms. The voice of God is powerful and full of majesty. All knowledge originates in him. Because he is exalted as head over all, greatness, power, glory, and victory belong to him.

You are precious to God. To trust him by placing your complete confidence and hope in him is to experience stepping into his presence and walking securely with him untouched by adversity. In God's presence is everything you could ever desire to move your life forward, prospering in any area of life. You were made by God to live in his presence and flourish.

In Genesis chapter 1, verse 26, God said, Let us make man in our image and after our likeness. Who is us? I believe it is God the Father, the Word of God who is Jesus Christ, his Son, and the Holy Spirit. Verse 27 says, So God created man in his own image, in the image of God created he him; male and female created he them. When God created the male, he also created the female.

God said, Let them have dominion, which means authority or power, over the fish, the fowl, and over every living thing that moves upon the earth. He also allowed them to have dominion over all the earth. He did not give you control over others, as some may think. Using this authority, they were to be fruitful, multiply, fill the earth, and subdue it. God saw everything he had made, and it was very good.

The words create and make are not the same, because create is accomplished in the spiritual realm. Then God formed man's body, which is his outer covering for his spirit and soul, from the dust of the ground. By the way, at that time, the earth was perfect and glorious. God breathed life into him, and he became a living soul. The man became a speaking spirit. Created, uniquely made, and filled by God with his attributes, mankind's spirit and soul were designed to be like him. Created in God's image means that your real self is a spirit who possesses a soul. Your spirit looks like you. The soul is your mind, will, emotions, intellect, and imagination, which are like God, but they are what makes you different from anyone else. The faculties of the mind also include reason, memory, intuition, and perception.

Each day, God himself taught the man how to develop and use each area of his soul. Briefly described, the man had the mind of God. God is divine, so he made the man divine. His free will, which allowed him to choose, was aligned in agreement with the will of God. With the intellect of God to access, the man was brilliant. He used his imagination to formulate his thoughts and combine them with the emotions of God's love. Feelings of joy and gladness, flowing from his heart, created what he imagined. He was made to live and function as God does.

God planted a garden on the east side of Eden. He made every tree that is pleasant to the sight and good for food to grow out of the ground. The tree of life was also in the midst of the garden, and the tree of knowledge of good and evil. God placed the man in the garden to work it and guard it. He told him he could freely eat from every tree in the garden, except one. With man's freedom of choice, came a warning. God told the man not to eat the fruit from the tree of the knowledge of good and evil. If he ate the fruit, the same day, he would surely die. God had given man eternal life. All man knew was the goodness of God's glory. To mix the pure knowledge of God with the knowledge of good and evil would cause him to lose eternal life and eventually die physically.

As the scripture said, God created and made man, male and female. He called the man Adam. Genesis chapter 2, verses 21 through 25, describe how God caused Adam to fall into a deep sleep, took one of his ribs, made the woman, and brought her to him. Adam said, this is now bone of my bones, and flesh of my flesh: she shall be called Woman, because she was taken out of Man. Adam did not mention her spirit and soul, but only their physical oneness. She had been created in God's image and after his likeness. Now God with a rib from man, as the scriptures say, God designed and made her. Her spirit and soul were unique to her as they are to each of you. They are what make you different from one another.

What were the man and the woman meant to accomplish with God's eternal life in them? The spiritual realm held no impossibilities for them because they were perfect, divine, and clothed in God's glory. They were meant to fill the earth with the knowledge of God's glory. In the authority God gave them, they were to follow God's mandate to be fruitful, multiply, replenish the earth and subdue it by reproducing the Garden of Eden throughout the earth. They were to use every herb bearing seed on the face of the earth and every fruit tree with a tree yielding seed. God's family was to learn and move in his word, power, and ways as they multiplied across the earth in their heritage of dominion. Living in God's presence, enjoying the goodness of his glory, was to be their way of life forever.

One day, God's enemy Satan, the fallen angel, presented the woman with an evil thought. He deceived her by suggesting that God was withholding the knowledge of good and evil from them that would open their eyes and make them as gods. He told her that if she ate the fruit, she would not surely die. The enemy uses three temptations repeatedly to sway humanity away from God. I John 2:16 says, For all that is in the world, the lust of the flesh, and the lust of the eyes, and the pride of life, is not of the Father, but is of the world. In Genesis 3:6, the woman saw that the tree was good for food and that it was pleasant to the eyes. It was a tree to be desired to make one wise. Deceived by Satan, she took the fruit and ate it. Then she gave it also to her husband with her, and he ate. The man, ignoring the warning from God, was not deceived.

With her husband's agreement, their actions against God allowed the curse of death to enter the earth. As a result, their decision caused them to die spiritually on the same day, and lose their glory covering. Physical death, which was never in God's plan for his family, came later.

God is love. He sent redemption from sin and death through his Son Jesus Christ. If you have chosen to close your eyes and ears to God's words and ways, you can open them. Deciding to receive Jesus Christ in your heart is one step away from the eternal life God has provided for you. The resurrection of the Lord Jesus Christ and his ascension to the right hand of the Father is the only living truth and proof of the promise of eternal life. The power of the resurrection to eternal life separates you from the abilities of man in his natural state. Learning how to draw on God's power, knowledge, and presence enables you to break free from the intricate connections that seek to control your life. It is up to you to receive God's ability and develop the potential he has given you.

If you are still waiting for God to do something about your life, he has sent his Son and his thoughts of redemption your way. Now, he is waiting for your response. To receive eternal life right now and all the good God has for you, with all sincerity, ask Jesus Christ to come into your heart.

I believe in my heart that God raised Jesus from the dead. I turn away from a life of sin. Jesus, come into my heart and make me brand new. Thank you.

PART 1: THE DECISION

Chapter 1

Summary Questions
&
Reference Scriptures

PART 1: THE DECISION
Chapter 1 Summary Questions

Are Your Decision-Making Abilities Hampered?
Cut the Strings of Adversity?

1. When you were a child, did you wonder about God?

2. Did you have a question about God that would have changed your life? Did you ask it?

3. What thought or situation keeps you from moving forward in an area of your life? How will you change it?

4. Each time you decide to make a change, do you experience thoughts of opposition?

5. What did the boy puppet do before he realized he could cut himself free?

6. What makes you aware that you are already free and can overcome manipulation?

7. In your opinion, do you live a prosperous life where you feel you do not need to progress? If so, why?

8. Why should I commit to God totally and place myself in his hands?

9. Who pulled the puppet's strings and manipulated his every move?

10. Do your circumstances make you feel stuck with no way out?

Chapter 1 Scripture References
Descriptive Notes Taken from the Scripture for Research

Eyes Closed, Ears Closed, Unbelief

Matthew 13:15
Their ears are dull of hearing, and they have closed their eyes.

II Corinthians 4:3-4
The god of this world has blinded the minds of those who do not believe.

God's Thoughts and Plans for You

Isaiah 55:7-11
Forsake your thoughts and ways. My word shall not return void.

Psalm 40:5
My God, your thoughts to us, are more than can be numbered.

Psalm 94:19
In the multitude of my thoughts within me, your comforts delight my soul.

Psalm 139:17
How also are your precious thoughts unto me, O God!

Jeremiah 29:11
For I know the thoughts I think toward you.

Make the LORD your God

Jeremiah 17:5-8
Blessed is the man that trusts in the LORD, whose hope the LORD is.

Who is God?

John 4:24
God is a Spirit.

I John 1:5
God is light, and in him is no darkness at all.

I John 4:8
God is love.

Isaiah 57:15
For thus says the high and lofty One that inhabits eternity, whose name is Holy.

I Timothy 1:17
To the King eternal, immortal, invisible, the only wise God, be honor and glory forever and ever. Amen.

I Chronicles 29:11-12
All that is in heaven and earth is thine. You reign over all.

Psalm 93:1
The LORD is clothed with majesty and strength.

Isaiah 66:1
The heaven is my throne, and the earth is my footstool.

Psalm 103:19
The LORD hath prepared his throne in the heavens; and his kingdom rules over all.

Psalm 29:4
The voice of the LORD is powerful; the voice of the LORD is full of majesty.

Souls Are Precious to God

Job 12:10
In whose hand is the soul of every living thing, and the breath of all mankind.

Psalm 49:7-9
The redemption of their soul is precious. He should still live forever.

Made in God's Image and after his Likeness

Genesis 1:26-28
God created man in his image and after his likeness.

Genesis 2:7
God formed man and breathed the breath of life into him.

Genesis 2:9
The LORD God made every tree that is pleasant to the sight, and good for food to grow.

Genesis 2:21-25
God made the woman and brought her to the man.

Man Loses Eternal Life

I John 2:16
The lust of the eyes, the lust of the flesh, and the pride of life is of the world.

Genesis 3:6
The woman ate the fruit. She gave it to her husband, and he ate it also.

I Timothy 2:14
Adam was not deceived, but the woman being deceived was in transgression.

Receive Jesus Christ in Your Heart

Romans 10:8-10
That if you confess with your mouth the Lord Jesus, and shall believe in your heart that God has raised him from the dead, you shall be saved.

CHAPTER 2

Stand without Manipulation

Freedom: The Real Option

The puppet is now standing on his own. God revealed himself to the young boy in a way that caused him to trust what he heard and take action. With the ability to listen to a different voice, he now desired to know more; to do more. Standing there, waiting, wondering what will happen next, but hearing nothing, he takes in a deep breath and slowly exhales. Freedom feels good. Holding his head up, on his own, he looks around and smiles. Noticing his hands, he holds them out in front of him, and then reaches up to touch his face, his hair, and then lifts his hat and places it back on his head. For the first time in a long time, he notices his clothes and especially his shoes. 'They're so dirty,' he thought sadly. 'I must look dirty and out of sorts. I didn't realize.'

Questions begin to flood his mind. What now? All he had ever known or thought to be true just changed. What was he supposed to do now? What will he need to learn to keep himself free from manipulation? Whatever it is, he has decided to find it, learn it, and live it. Listening again, he hears nothing. "Will God speak to me again," he asks himself, "or am I on my own? Is this feeling of relief all there is to freedom, or is there more? There has to be more!" Wondering, he thinks, 'What should I do now?'

He lifts one leg straight up and puts it down. He lifts the other leg straight up and puts it down. Then he lifts his arms even with his waist to balance himself, leans slightly forward and gingerly takes his very first step. Still standing, wondering if he should take another step, he hears God asks him a question, "Where are you going?" Startled, but glad to hear God's voice again, he stops to answer him. "I don't know. I feel like I have to do something; either go somewhere far away from here or maybe, I should stay." After a pause, God asks, "How will you get somewhere from here if you don't know where you are going?" He says, "I don't know. I just found out I could move."

God addresses his second choice by saying, "Are you strong enough to stay here in what is familiar to you?" The boy replies, "Strong enough? I don't think so." He didn't know what he didn't know, so he didn't know how to answer the question. He hears, "Do you think you can stay here and remain free of manipulation?" The puppet's response is, "No." God gives him the opportunity of his young life by asking, "Would you like to learn what you don't know?" With excitement, the young boy said, "Yes!" God begins by making a statement and then asking him another question. "The first step to learning something new is to see the things around you in a different way. What do you see?" he asks. The reply is, "I see my hands and my dirty clothes. Everything around me seems the same." Then God says, "Close your eyes. Now, what do you see?" The boy replies, "Nothing. No, wait! I see a glimmer of light!" God's response to him is, "Good! We can start there!"

No longer controlled by the unseen negative forces of the puppet master that kept him captive and manipulated, he now chose to listen to and follow the voice that helped him free himself. Two choices had come to his mind. Even though he has cut himself loose, he knows the oppressor is still present. To remain free, he must decide to leave and begin a new life in a new place or change the circumstances where he lives. Whatever he chooses to do, he knows that his strength, knowledge, confidence, courage, and direction must come from the one who has the power, the skill, and the experience to help him. To stay where he is and change his environment, he has to be strong enough to stay there while learning from God the ins and outs of living and remaining free of manipulation. The answer for him to come alive was God showing him how to remove the attachments of manipulative oppression when he could not hear or see for himself so he could understand.

Freedom is the real option. Becoming aware that you are living your life by the dictates of others, or from past experiences is an eye-opener. Deciding to break free of these unseen elements that hinder you from living the life God desires for you is a choice. Choose to believe the Word of God! There is no condemnation in Christ Jesus when you walk after the Spirit and not after what man thinks. Why, because the law of the Spirit of life in Christ Jesus hath made you free from the law of sin and death.

What is condemnation? In chapter 1, you read how mankind, male and female, was created and made to live eternally in the glorious presence of God. The ramifications of the curse of sin and death allowed to enter the earth through Adam's treason, and the deception of the woman by Satan was catastrophic. To live life continually dealing with the oppression of suffering, sickness, disabilities, poverty, abuse, and or any lack, etc., is solvable and changeable. When you know how to live by the law of the Spirit of life in Christ Jesus, you remain healed and free of oppression. When Jesus Christ redeemed humanity from the penalty of sin through his death, burial, and resurrection, he provided all of us with a choice. You can choose to live and once again walk after the Spirit of God or remain in condemnation. It is entirely our choice to freely make.

The young boy puppet decided to change his life by trusting God, and so can you. To move forward from here, you cannot allow condemning thoughts, words, and actions from yourself or others to control your life. If you do, you will continue to wait, stepping in place, marking time where you are. Living free in God's presence is to be able to be, do, and have the desires of his heart and yours. Living, learning, and walking after the Spirit of God is a life-changing journey!

To live by the law of the Spirit of Life in Christ Jesus, you must develop unshakable confidence in God. Transitioning to fully accept freedom from the oppression of condemnation to living in spiritual freedom in Christ Jesus is truly a faith walk. What is faith? Faith is your confidence in God that he will bring his Word to pass in your life. God reveals his ways to you as you grow spiritually to trust him from one level of faith to the next. Jesus grew God's faith in his life to the point of trusting his Father to resurrect him from hell and the grave. Receiving the ability to carry out the decisions you make through to the end, requires constant reinforcement of your connection and confidence in God's almighty power, infinite knowledge, and omnipresence.

Whether you decide to stay and change the circumstances where you are or move forward to begin a new life, challenges are always present. How you deal with these challenges depends on whether you have decided to trust yourself, someone else, or God. Putting your complete faith in God, rather than have your trust manipulated and misplaced for you, may sound new to you. Take the reins and make decisions for yourself, or someone else will try to make them for you. There will be times of change when pressure will confront you with the opportunity to revert to what is familiar because it feels comfortable. But you must learn to take control by deciding to trust God at all times. Only then can you consistently move forward.

Before the first airplane lifted off the ground and flew, no one believed it was possible because although the thought was received, their perception was that only birds were meant to fly. They refused to grasp the idea and associate it with people because they couldn't 'see' how people could fly through the air. Remember, God asked the boy what did he see, and the boy said, 'Nothing. No, wait! I see a glimmer of light!' People looked to themselves only to figure out if it could be true. God had already released the forces involved to fly the airplane when he made the heaven and the earth. They existed before anyone received the thought of man flying in a wooden or steel container as birds flew in the sky.

The four forces involved which allow the aircraft to take off and fly a straight and level flight are gravity (weight), lift, thrust and, drag. These forces already existed in the earth realm, but people were not aware of them. They couldn't see them, nor did they know as yet to seek them out. The forces God created for mankind to discover were not there by accident. As people became aware of them and sought God for answers, God didn't disappoint. For the airplane to fly, lift works equally to or opposite of gravity. Thrust works equally to or opposite of drag.

Just as these forces work to overcome or complement each other, you have to fight the unseen forces of negativity to change your perspective to God's heart perspective. If you allow gravity and drag (negative connections) to grow larger than lift and thrust (God's heart perspective), you will succumb to the norm and turn back to the company and conversation of the crowd. The possibility of an exciting new life must lift you, and the power of God's promises must thrust you up and out to a new life with Christ in God.

You'll Never Be Lonely Again

One evening, years ago, I was invited to a gathering in downtown San Diego at the Civic Center. A well-known evangelist was preaching there at a crusade. I had never been to this type of church service. Not knowing what to expect other than hearing some preaching, I followed my friend inside and found a seat. I had never seen so many people so excited to be in a place without cheerleaders and ball teams. For me, church service had always been very dull. It was a place my family went to on Sunday to socialize, sing, and hear about God. I enjoyed the socializing and the singing to a point, but the sermons were excruciatingly dull. These people waited with such anticipation for the crusade to begin. Why?

The service proceeded as I expected with music and then the introduction of the speaker. It wasn't long before I realized that I had never heard the Word of God preached in such a manner. All I felt was the love of God and real hope for a better life. When he suddenly proclaimed, "If you accept Jesus into your heart, you'll never be lonely again!" I was done in! I had to have this.

For several reasons during my childhood and teenage years, including being constantly bullied, my heart had felt empty for a long time. Even though my experiences with God were many, I felt the need to keep them to myself because I didn't think people would understand. Friendships were few. There were always conversations and visions from God happening on the inside of me about various people I knew. I couldn't share them, because how would I have known these things ahead of time in the first place? The lack of perceived opportunities available to share my God experiences with anyone took a toll on me. Eventually, I became a person who sought love and the friendship of people rather than my relationship with God. Although the prior knowledge of situations before they happened and the visions continued, my heart had emptied itself because I needed the friendships of people I could touch. Instead of a God pleaser, I became a people pleaser.

Now, even though I didn't understand what had happened to me in the crusade, I returned to the Methodist church, determined to find someone who could help me live this love of Jesus in my heart. To my dismay, I couldn't find anyone who knew about salvation by inviting Jesus Christ into your heart. To them, joining a church and attending service was all they had to do. I was made to feel like I had done something wrong by going to the crusade in the first place. I had a choice. I could choose to stay at the Methodist church where nothing had changed, or I could leave. There were no bible studies. I was only aware of the little Sunday school bible stories I had heard growing up in my home town. Was there any hope for me that I would listen to someone speak the powerful words I heard at the crusade or experience anything close to it again? I thought not!

Continuing to hear the familiar sermons of my past while trying to survive on my lack of Bible knowledge held little or no hope for me to survive the onslaught of negative voices directed at me from family members and others. Before this, at most, people only said hello to me. I didn't know what I didn't know, but I knew that I was right to choose Jesus Christ! With assurance in my heart that God had more for me, I knew I could follow him to a new place. What was my strategy? I needed to reestablish my close relationship with him and learn to live my life the way he intended. What did I choose? I chose to follow God!

To see above and beyond what others call normal, changing your perspective to God's heart perspective is necessary. It's easy to follow the well-worn paths of the majority. There you'll find plenty of company, easy conversation, and nostalgic scenery. Fish travel in schools, birds travel in formations, and animals run in herds, but man was made like God to excel in every area of life with him. Stepping out of the majority to travel in a new direction, usually causes friction from the participants. They fail to understand your reasoning to turn aside, even though you repeatedly explain your 'unique' views to them in a variety of ways. Nothing will satisfy them because leaving the familiarity of the crowd to follow an 'unknown' path, makes you different from them.

To weather the storm of their unbelief, and rise above it, you have to pay the price within yourself to stay strong in God's love. With Jesus in your heart, you have the assurance of God's love and his willingness to direct your life. Learning to follow God up a new path will always be new to you. To see in the spirit, hear God's voice, take steps in uncharted territory, or even feel this good about yourself means that you are lifting off up above the crowd. In the past, your decisions and movements were out of your control. They kept you bowed down, running low to the ground with the illusion of flying. Now, with your eyes open, your perspective has changed.

Whether you decide to move forward or stay where you are, you should focus your thinking on God's thoughts only. Negative or stagnant thoughts will always try to keep you in their thought patterns with the power of comfort and familiarity. If you let them, they'll stifle your ability to consider his thoughts for any length of time. Making your way mentally past this negativity remains difficult as long as you depend on yourself to accomplish it. Looking at what you desire to change, but continuing to see what is, will not change a thing. The thoughts you feel and believe to be real with applied actions determine what you speak and do daily. Changing what you experience in your life requires that you first change what you receive and see in your imagination. As the negative thoughts come to mind, refuse to consider them. Choose not to engage them. To allow these thoughts to form into pictures and sentences only strengthen the negative patterns of thinking and the feelings that are already working against you. Let negative thoughts float away before familiar unwanted feelings begin to surface.

How do you know what God's heart perspective is in any given situation? Ask him, relax, and receive the answer in your spirit. You are not to rush the solution by allowing thoughts to swirl in your mind. If the answer sounds like what you would typically do in that situation, it's probably not God's answer. There are more thoughts directed to you from God than you could ever imagine. Make his thoughts precious to you. Be assured; he has already answered. Patiently receive his response by listening, or by calmly looking to see his answer in your spirit. To make it up by yourself out of nervousness or thinking he doesn't care shows a lack of trust. Then do or say what he gives you.

Dissipating the manipulative voices and sounds of the mental and emotional fog of confusion that affects everything you say and do, is just the beginning. To change who controls your environment, you must not only change how you think and feel but what you believe. Doing this will help you manage your emotions and how you respond to others. You can choose to think negative thoughts and remain in adversity or replace them with God's thoughts and ways. To keep yourself free from the intricate negative connections of people who would desire to control your thoughts, feelings, beliefs, and actions, give yourself permission to make this change. It is your choice, no one else's.

PART 1: THE DECISION

Chapter 2

Summary Questions

&

Reference Scriptures

PART 1: THE DECISION
Chapter 2 Summary Questions

Stand without Manipulation
Freedom: The Real Option

1. How can you tell if you are being manipulated by others in certain areas of our life?

2. Do you know how to ask God what to do to change your thinking in these areas?

3. What does eternal life mean to you?

4. Are you aware of the freedom the law of the Spirit of life in Christ Jesus has provided for you?

5. Choices confront us every day. When you choose to change directions with God, are you aware of the challenges you may face from yourself or others?

6. Have you changed your perspective to God's heart perspective? How do you know that you have?

7. Can you genuinely say that you hear the voice of God? Explain how you know they are his thoughts.

8. Do you take the time to learn from God and act on what you hear?

Chapter 2 Scripture References
Descriptive Notes for Research

Free from the Law of Sin and Death

Romans 8:1-2
There is now no condemnation to them which are in Christ Jesus.

Acts 10:38
Jesus went about doing good, and healing all that were oppressed of the devil.

Living by Faith

Romans 1:17
The just shall live by faith.

Galatians 2:20
The life which I now live in the flesh I live by the faith of the Son of God.

Jesus Raised from the Dead by the Glory of God

Romans 6:4-6
Christ was raised up from the dead by the glory of the Father.

Make God's Thoughts Precious

Psalm 139:17
How precious also are your thoughts unto me, O God!

Confidence in God

I John 5:14-15
This is the confidence that we have in him that, if we ask any thing according to his will, he hears us.

PART 2: THE PURPOSE

Freedom

CHAPTER 3

Your First Step of Freedom
The Realization of 'Empty' Space

With his decision made to rise above what others call normal to follow God, the boy puppet has progressed from seeing nothing to placing all his hope in him. With his first step of freedom comes the realization of 'empty' space filled with a sigh of timeless pause. Even though he can't explain it, he knows there has been a wonderful change. His clothes are fresh and clean. He can see himself in his polished wooden shoes. He reaches up to touch his face, then runs his fingers through his hair. His cheeks feel soft to the touch, and his hair feels good, sliding through his fingers. Then he lifts his hat to look at the feather. It's straight. The colorful feathers are holding their own in the warm breeze. He places his hat back on his head, closes his eyes, and lets out a sigh of relief. Opening them, he smiles. No longer is he a dirty puppet boy with no hope. For the first time, he feels light-hearted and clean. Peace and joy have flooded him so profoundly that he knows he has to have more. At all costs, he never wants to lose this feeling of freedom. The boy's questions are, 'How do I keep feeling this good? How do I stay here? What do I do now? Where is my life going, and how do I get there from here?' What he does not realize 'in' this moment is that he is standing in the presence of God.

In the greatness of the omnipresence of God is glory, honor, and fullness of joy. His infinite glory is the eternal beauty of all he is. God covers himself with light like a garment. This light is illumination in every sense, including lightning, happiness, brilliance, purity, life, prosperity, truth and its knowledge, instruction, heavenly, daylight, etc. In his timeless presence, the past, present, and future are ever before you. All there ever was and ever will be is now. God, in his omnipresence, hears, sees, and knows all.

When God asked the boy puppet what he saw, at first, he said, 'Nothing.' Then, he saw a glimmer of light. How is this possible for you? When God raised Jesus from the dead, he raised you from the dead with him, delivering you from the power of darkness and translating you into the kingdom of Jesus Christ. With Jesus Christ in your heart, you are spiritually alive. Now for you, all things are of God. God created and made the heavens and the earth. Jesus Christ redeemed everything in heaven and on earth, including you. This change of spiritual position potentially changes everything in your life for you. You, like the young boy, now recognize the light of God's presence in you and all around you because you are in his kingdom, the realm of heaven. You are standing in that realm of heaven and on earth in the same moment.

How do you recognize the change? Your spirit man has come alive, and your heart is full of joy and peace because it's full of God's love. By the power of the Holy Spirit, your spirit, soul, and body are spiritually brand new. You may only recognize the joy and the peace you feel in your heart, but as far as God is concerned, your spirit and soul, which are the real you, have been reborn unto eternal life. Colossians 3, verses 9 and 10 refer to the former you as the old man and the new you as the new man. You have put off the dead man with his old ways, and have put on the new man who is spiritually alive in Christ Jesus. II Corinthians chapter 5, verse 17, says the former things of the old man are passed away. They no longer have control over you unless you give them access by agreeing with them in thought, word, and action. All spiritual things have become new for you. Your spirit, soul, and body are now spiritually aligned with God.

Do you realize how powerful your alignment with God is? Look at the life of Jesus Christ. His health, wealth, wisdom, success, and actions were perfectly aligned with God's desires because he sought after his Father's will in prayer continuously. His ministry of reconciliation, which included destroying the works of the devil, was his purpose on earth. No matter how much you pursue after God and his goodness, there is always more. All of this is available to you right now! What is the purpose of this powerful alignment with God, Jesus Christ, and the Holy Spirit? The ultimate answer found in Revelation chapter 11, verse 15 says, the kingdoms of this world are become the kingdoms of our Lord, and of his Christ; and he shall reign for ever and ever.

As far as God is concerned, the spiritual realm is reality. The kingdoms of this enemy-controlled world have already become the kingdoms of the Lord God and Jesus Christ. The Lord Jesus Christ shall reign for ever and ever. The earth has to catch up. What do you think will happen? Will the earth replace heaven, or will the events follow Matthew chapter 6, verse 10 says, your kingdom come. Your will be done in earth, as it is in heaven. Learning how to follow God's lead is essential to carry out his will in the earth.

With your permission, the former things of your soul allowed others to control you, mentally and physically. These things are how the boy puppet succumbed to the power and decisions of the puppet master. He could not see, hear, think, speak, move, or do anything for himself. Spiritual blindness, caused by unbelief in God, resulted in his lack of knowledge. This combination allowed the puppet master to feel secure in his absolute control.

The boy's mannerism was the result of his depressed, helpless state, reinforced by emotional pain.

For you, living life in the kingdom of the Lord Jesus Christ allows you to experience immersion in God's glory full of love, joy, peace, wisdom, power, and all that he is. Right now, your life is hidden with Christ in God because God is your Father. You are no longer a servant of sin, but you are an heir of God through Christ. Learning to see, hear, think, speak, move, or do anything in the spiritual realm is taught and accomplished by the Spirit of the Lord from God's heart perspective. Colossians chapter 2, verse10 says, you are complete in him, which is the head of all principality and power. With your eyes open, you have God's ability to access and discover his goodness. Hearing his voice more clearly enables you to make the right choices. In him, you live, move, and have your being. Filled with the presence of God, you think as God thinks, say what he says, and do what he shows you. No longer a citizen of the earth, you are now a citizen of heaven with a heavenly conversation. Your physical body is on the earth, but your spirit and soul willingly belong to God.

To change from total manipulation to receiving all the goodness God has for you requires that you trust his movements and follow his lead in everything. Deciding to allow God to guide you in all that you do is a lifelong commitment? You are a joint heir with Jesus Christ of all the spiritual and natural things he has redeemed. The realization of all these things is complete in heaven, but not on earth. Most people who have invited Jesus Christ into their hearts, becoming rightful heirs to what salvation is, which is deliverance from sin and its consequences, provides for them, do not pursue their possessions. They live as if Jesus never redeemed them or all the spiritual and natural things for them. Here, where you stand, you have never-ending access to all Jesus has redeemed and to what God has planned for you. He will show you the path of life as you follow his lead. Unlimited possibilities are now awaiting your unwavering choice and attention.

To become aware of and see these unlimited possibilities requires a change of perspective, which results in a changed perception of your surroundings. In the past, you were dominated and led by your soul, which was influenced and controlled by the enemy. No longer is your body under the control of your soul first and then your unregenerate spirit. Now the Holy Spirit is teaching you how to be led by your spirit into the freedom of knowing God's love, mercy, power, and grace. You are now spirit, soul, and then the body, in that order.

Standing in the midst of eternal life, love, and light, the glory of God changes your perspective on a grand scale. To see, think, speak, and act from this new perspective draws you into new perceptions of what is possible for you to accomplish, become, and obtain, whether it is spiritual or natural. Preparation is needed to navigate from your old spirit man to your new spirit man, who is one with God. Your soul, which resides in your spirit, is what makes you unique from anyone else. The dictates of your soul controlled your old spirit man but were never meant to control your new spirit man. The development of your soul, which includes your mind, will, emotions, intellect, imagination, intuition, reason, memory, and perception, aligns with your spirit to follow the lead of the Holy Spirit. The Holy Spirit leads you because your spirit, soul, and body now belong to God.

How does the Holy Spirit lead you? He guides you into all truth. To cooperate with him means hearing, seeing, and speaking God's Word as he gives it to you. All things that belong to the Father belong to Jesus Christ. You are an heir of God and a joint-heir with Jesus Christ. Colossians chapter 2, verse 3, says, all the treasures of wisdom and knowledge are hid in God and Christ. Verse 10 of Colossians chapter 2 says you are complete in him, which is the head of all principality and power. The Holy Spirit speaks to you what he hears from Jesus. Receiving spiritual things from him, he shows them to you. By doing this, he shows you the things that are still to come in your life or events that will happen.

For this reason, it is vitally important that you become determined to live life from your spirit. Through the knowledge of God and Jesus Christ, you will experience increase, multiplication, restoration, and so much more. The Spirit of the Lord changes you with your permission into the image of Jesus Christ from glory to glory. Take steps to learn from the Holy Spirit. He teaches you, shows, and guides you on how to exercise your dominion to progress in life spiritually and naturally.

Following the Holy Spirit on the path God has chosen for you begins by endeavoring to hear his voice more clearly, and having the ability to see what he says. When you follow his directions, you will begin to understand differently. Listening to the thoughts of God is to see the words as they relate to you. When God speaks to you by his Spirit or shows you a scripture to read, seeing the words will cause them to come alive in picture form. For now, you are to train yourself not to consider them as they relate to others, but only how they relate to you. Doing this does not mean that others are wrong in their beliefs. It means that you have chosen to go spiritually deeper with God and are allowing him to take you higher with him. Beginning to walk in this freedom opens more opportunities for you to see and obtain unlimited possibilities to progress in him and with him.

Your imagination will create scenes from the thoughts that come to you because of how you associate the words you hear with how you see. The same thing happens when someone says to a group of people, 'I see each of you riding a horse.' Instantly, moving scenes begin to come together in their imaginations. If asked, each person in the group would describe a different realistic scenario in living color. Allowing themselves to linger in the scene will cause them to feel the movement of the horse under their seat in the saddle. Holding the reins loosely in their hands, feeling the breeze on their faces, and riding along a trail at a gallop would seem very real. The reality of each of their creative film clips would convince them that theirs was the best scene created.

Breaking away from familiarity causes you to assess your emotions and feelings immediately. Even though your mind is made up, everything you've ever known as reality has to change or catch up. Your feelings are no exception. Most people allow their emotions to tell them what to do. If they feel good, they believe they will have a good day. If they've given in to non-complacent feelings, anger, or sadness, they think their day will not go so well. How you perceive a thing or situation is to change how you feel, not the other way around.

Because you are in Christ Jesus, and he is in God, you have the ability to discover the unlimited possibilities which are already in you. Because you are complete in him, the presence, power, and knowledge of God are already in you. Look, expecting to see, acknowledge, and uncover his goodness of God in you. Look means to look in the spirit realm. Where is the spiritual realm? It is in you and all around you. Acknowledge means to accept or admit the existence or truth of something. Where are the limitless possibilities? Philemon chapter 1, verse 6, tells you to acknowledge every good thing which is in you in Christ Jesus. Once the Holy Spirit shows you a possibility, recognize it by imaging it and then believe in the reality of it for yourself. The Holy Spirit will guide you to search out the truth of it. It is your responsibility to apply it to your daily life. Learning to manifest these limitless possibilities by faith will not only change your life but can lead to improving the lives of others as well.

The Holy Spirit will show you how to navigate from the 'empty' space where you stand, to where you desire to go, who you wish to become, and what you want to obtain. What seemed to be 'empty' space was never empty. Because you were renewed in knowledge after the image of God, what God desires for your life, is already manifest in you. Romans chapter 1, verse 19, says because that which may be known of God is manifest in them; for God hath showed it to them. Verse 20 states for the invisible things of him from the creation of the world are clearly seen, being understood by the things that are made, even his eternal power and Godhead; so that they are without excuse. You can understand the invisible things created and made by God. They are clearly seen now and understood because you can see them manifested on the earth. God's eternal Godhead and power created and made all things. The Holy Spirit shows you the things God has planned for you in your spirit. As you seek him about them, he reveals the truth to you in the scripture concerning them. Then as you move into what he has taught you by applying his Word to your life, change takes place, resulting in the manifestation of the desires of your heart.

PART 2: THE PURPOSE
Chapter 3

Summary Questions
&
Reference Scriptures

PART 2: THE PURPOSE
Chapter 3 Summary Questions

Your First Step of Freedom
The Realization of 'Empty' Space

1. Have you experienced the presence of God? Describe your experience.

2. Do you realize how powerful your alignment with God is?

3. What part has God given you to help bring about his ultimate purpose described in Revelation 11:15?

4. Are you allowing the Holy Spirit to teach you from God's heart perspective?

5. What does becoming a citizen of heaven mean to you?

6. Have you given thought to what unlimited possibilities mean for you?

7. Why are you now spirit, soul, and body instead of body, soul, and spirit?

8. Do you have an active part in the development of your soul?

9. Are you living your life in spiritual freedom with the Holy Spirit?

10. How has Chapter 3 changed your perspective and perception?

Chapter 3 Scripture References
Descriptive Notes Taken from the Scripture for Research

In the Presence of God

Psalm 16:11
You will show me the path of life: in your presence is fullness of joy.

Psalm 140:13
The righteous shall give thanks to your name: the upright shall dwell in your presence.

I Chronicles 16:27
Glory and honor are in his presence; strength and gladness are in his place.

God Covers Himself with Light

Psalm 104:1-2
You are very great, clothed with honor and majesty; you cover yourself in light.

Proverbs 16:15
In the light of the king's countenance is life.

I John 1:5
God is light, and in him is no darkness at all.

Christ Lives in Me

Galatians 2:20
I am crucified with Christ: nevertheless I live; yet not I, but Christ lives in me.

Colossians 1:12-15
The Father has delivered us from the power of darkness, and has translated us into the kingdom of his dear Son.

II Corinthians 5:17
Therefore if any man be in Christ, he is a new creature: old things are passed away; behold, all things are become new.

Romans 15:13
Now the God of hope fill you with all joy and peace in believing, that you may abound in hope, through the power of the Holy Ghost.

In the Kingdom of Jesus Christ

I John 3:8
For this purpose the Son of God was manifested, that he might destroy the works of the devil.

Revelation 11:15
The kingdoms of this world are become the kingdoms of our Lord, and of his Christ; and he shall reign for ever and ever.

Matthew 6:10
Your kingdom come, your will be done in earth, as it is in heaven.

II Corinthians 4:4-5
The god of this world hath blinded the minds of them which believe not.

Colossians 1: 13
Who has delivered us from the power of darkness, and has translated us into the kingdom of his dear Son.

Colossians 3:3
For you are dead, and your life is hid with Christ in God.

Romans 8:16-17
We are the children of God: heirs of God, and joint-heirs with Christ.

Acts 17:28
For in him we live, and move, and have our being. We are his offspring.

Ephesians 2:18-19
You are fellow citizens with the saints, and of the household of God.

Philippians 3:20
Our conversation is in heaven.

Expect to See the Goodness of God

Psalm 27:13
I had fainted, unless I had believed to see the goodness of the LORD in the land of the living.

Philemon 1:6
Acknowledging of every good thing which is in you in Christ Jesus.

Led of the Holy Spirit

Colossians 3:8-10
You have put off the old man with his deeds, and have put on the new man, which is renewed in knowledge after the image of him that created him.

II Peter 1:2
Grace and peace be multiplied unto you through the knowledge of God, and of Jesus our Lord.

John 5:19-20
The Son can do nothing of himself, but what he sees the Father do.

John 8:28
I do nothing of myself; but as my Father hath taught me, I speak these things.

John 16:13-15
The Spirit of truth will guide you into all truth, and he will shew you things to come.

Colossians 2:2-3
To the acknowledgement of the mystery of God, and of the Father, and of Christ; in whom are hid all the treasures of wisdom and knowledge.

Colossians 2:9-10
For in him dwells all the fullness of the Godhead bodily. You are complete in him, which is the head of all principality and power.

II Corinthians 3:17-18
We all are changed into the same image from glory to glory, by the Spirit of the Lord.

CHAPTER 4

Stepping Into Unlimited Possibilities

The Two-Way Open-Ended Lens

Standing in the midst of God's eternal life, love, and light, has changed the puppet boy's perspective. The Spirit of God quickened him, giving him life from the blindness of one dimension, opening his eyes to the three dimensions of his spirit, soul, and body. Resetting him 180 degrees and activating his spiritual senses made him aware of his new connection from the third dimension to the fourth dimension, where he stands in God's eternal life, love, and light. God's goodness created such expectation for him that his eyes opened to the unlimited possibilities God had previously planned for his life. Desiring to see, know, and experience more, the puppet who formerly could do nothing on his own, has now received the revelation that his first step of freedom was freedom itself. Accepting the resetting and lifting of his perspective 180 degrees, changed the direction of his life. Realizing that true freedom is not maneuvering on his own, but is trusting the Holy Spirit to lead him, he decides to make the necessary spiritual changes to pursue and obtain the possibilities God desires for his life.

How are you able to live and change your life with such a powerful, all-knowing God? God is a Spirit. Psalm 82, verse 6, and John chapter 10, verse 34 both say, you are gods. Made in God's image and after his likeness, as deity over the earth, you were meant to rule with him. You are a spirit with a soul who lives in a spiritual body. Your soul, which reflects you at any given moment, is used in many ways to assist you, whether personally, corporately, or environmentally to carry out God's command. From the beginning, God blessed you and commanded you to be fruitful, multiply, replenish the earth, and subdue it by exercising your dominion. Like God, you create your reality in the spiritual realm. Then, if allowed by you, this new reality changes how you live your life on the earth.

When you received Jesus Christ in your heart, God quickened you together with Christ, then raised you up and made you sit together in heavenly places or realms. Where is the Lord Jesus Christ seated? He is seated in heavenly places at God's right hand far above all principality, power, might, dominion, and every name that is named. He is seated above every name in this world and also in the world to come. Since Jesus is seated at God's right hand, which means having a special place of honor, in him, so are you. God's right hand refers to his omnipotent power, authority, strength, blessing, protection, salvation, provision, promise, and sovereignty. From this seated position, you are to work with God through him to fulfill his purpose for you in heaven and on earth. Unless by his sovereignty and grace, he chooses to act on your behalf concerning blessing you or protecting you from something you are unaware of, he expects you to grow spiritually by following his lead.

Becoming aware of and stepping into what is available to you since the death, burial, and resurrection of Jesus Christ reveals the marvelous opportunities that await you. Making God your source to receive all that pertains to life and godliness is just the beginning. He expects you to exercise your dominion with him to affect the things the two of you desire to subdue, change, multiply, replenish, replace, or create in your lifetime on earth.

You are a citizen of heaven, which means that you live in the heavenly realm, even as your body is on the earth. To affect change on earth, you must first learn from the Holy Spirit how to live from your spirit and soul. God, in his sovereignty, is absolute. To wherever and whatever he sends his Word, it prospers. His thoughts, spoken words, and his way of doing things always nourish, cause growth, and accomplish specific results for those who are willing to receive from him and repeat the process his way. The Lord has preeminence over all things in heaven and the earth because he created all things visible and invisible. His preeminence is good news for you because as joint-heirs with him, you already have what you desire.

Viewing life through a two-way open-ended lens reveals an enormous expanse of the available unlimited possibilities of heaven as well as humanity's changeable limitations on the earth. Changeable is the keyword. Heavenly things are eternal and unchangeable. Spoken into existence by God himself, they cannot change or be changed unless he changes them. God spoke light out of the darkness. He divided the light from the darkness, and then he called the light Day and the darkness Night. Day and Night still stand. Seated in the heavenly realm, you speak unchangeable, eternal things into existence out of life, love, and light. God is eternal life. His love is unconditional. In him is light and no darkness at all. God gave Jesus life, and in him, you can create out of life, love, and light with your thoughts and spoken words.

What are these changeable things? They are whatever you desire to change for the good. They are not only the wrong things but are the good things that can be made better, including material things stemming from the ideas you settle for because you believe the words of other people without using your right to challenge how they arrived at their conclusion. Who are these other people? They are your parents, well-meaning friends, the majority, religious and social leaders, self-made experts, teachers, scientists, doctors, and other authority figures who tell you there is nothing that can change a particular outcome. They say, 'There is no hope. We've always done it this way. You can't do that because no one like you has ever done that! You'll never change or be good for anything other than what you are doing right now. Who do you think you are anyway?'

I call them the 'they people.' The 'they people' are in charge of keeping you in your place or holding you down from believing for yourself. Some other ways used to influence your life are Hollywood stars who are only playing a part, news media who only report what someone else tells them to say. Questionable decisions that you would not otherwise make because you listened to songs with suggestive lyrics, good or bad, and captivating music. Articles, history books, pictures, commercials, and other sensory stimulators that are not necessarily true for your life or relevant. All of these thoughts, spoken words, along with their results, can be counteracted by your thoughts, spoken words, and actions. It's what you see, think, and say over your life that changes it. It's the actions you take, not you giving in and settling according to what others say about you.

The elements of life enfolded in the systematic way of the world on earth vary in range from your personal life to society, to corporate, to environmental. Personally, the areas available for development and change are spiritual, mental, physical, financial, and social. People feel powerless in these areas concerning health problems, lack of any kind, and social separation arises when their conditioning tells them there is nothing they can do about it. Corporately, areas in different forms include family, education, religion, economic, government, media, the arts, and entertainment. These are the main areas of society in which each field contains intricate variations within. People from all walks of life through the power of awareness and knowledge are to take advantage of opportunities presented to them, good or bad and manifest the unlimited possibilities of heaven to advance in the areas of their choice.

Why do only a small percentage of people excel in these areas? Issues stemming from unfair competition, emotional problems, lack of education, controlled initiatives, and unbelief, to name a few, take the upper hand through suppression, oppression, and manipulation. The environment of the planet and its weather systems affect the air you breathe, the water you drink, and the condition of the land where you live. The animal, vegetable, and mineral kingdoms directly depend on the earth's environment. Control of the systematically strategic areas and regions of personal life, society, corporate, and the environment are expecting you to recognize their spiritual restoration in Christ and restore them to the kingdom of God on earth.

As stated in Chapter 1, your soul is your mind, will, emotions, intellect, and imagination. The faculties of the mind also include reason fueled by right thinking, memory, intuition, and perception. The multifaceted functions of your soul allow recognition, reason, and discernment of God's thoughts versus your thoughts. Renewed in knowledge after God, your new man has access to his intellect. Realizing the difference between his views and yours, deciding which ones to accept and receive as your own is not easy if you have not developed the elements of your soul.

How are your desired changes accomplished? Your spirit is one with the Spirit of God who is all-powerful, all-knowing, and is present everywhere. Changing your life begins in your spirit, then your soul, which is the turnstile to your body. As part of your soul, you have a conscious mind and a subconscious mind. Some things that influence and change the conscious mind are thoughts, pictures, and ideas of others. Other ways to learn and believe are hearing spoken words, music with emotional lyrics, how something affects your emotions, and the actions of others. The best way to learn anything is from the Holy Spirit, who passes knowledge to you or answers your questions with God's intellect. If accepted, and dwelled upon until it is considered correct and valid, the subconscious mind receives it as truth. To continue the process from not knowing to accomplish or mastering a skill, for example, is to become adept at it. Then, with practice, you become skillful at performing the task without consciously thinking about the process, step by step.

Compare this process to the act of learning to tie your shoes, beginning from not knowing what shoes and shoestrings are to quickly tying your shoes without much thought or mental effort on your part. You used your memory and imagination to remember how someone showed you how to tie your shoes. Your will is the same one you used to will the coordination of your fingers, your eyes to find the hole in the loop, and the right length of the shoestring and pressure to complete the task. The emotions you dealt with until you mastered tying your shoes are the same ones you deal with when you learn something new. Mastering your emotions is very important. You can grasp new things more quickly when you do not allow negative emotions to cause frustration.

What do I mean by your soul is the turnstile? Purposely aligning your spirit and soul to receive specific thoughts from God from his Word or his voice, initiate changes in your soul because your mind accepts them as the truth. Thinking the truth of God's Word in your conscious mind generates his thoughts in power to your subconscious mind, where you use your imagination to see and imagine the reality of the desired result. By using your imagination, you allow the emotion of God's love to envelop the vision of the result with full-fledged feelings of joy. Use the truth you have chosen as if your desired outcome is your usual way of life. If you do not believe the truth of God's Word changed your life, and you begin to give in to opposing thoughts, thinking, speaking, giving in to negative emotions, and acting on them, you have disconnected from your desired result. These things block the turnstile, and keep you stuck where you are.

Focusing on, imagining, and then speaking these specific thoughts releases them to create experiences that affect change in your physical body and or your situations and circumstances. The physical body, where outward actions take place, responds to the progressive knowledge, power, and presence of God you have allowed your spirit and soul to receive. Step by step at first, and then exponentially, you allow God to increase his presence, knowledge, and ability in you to change your life and surroundings.

Your love or concern for another person cannot make them change their life. You cannot do the work within them to change how they think. If that person desires a better life, he or she must receive in their spirit and do the mental and emotional work themselves from beginning to end by faith, trusting in God's Word Just as you have a free will, that person has a free will. The Holy Spirit speaks to you Words he has heard from Jesus Christ and shows you the things that are to come beforehand. Maintaining the vision and the feelings as your new normal, you learn that what the Holy Spirit reveals and teaches you is essential to applying what you have chosen to your life. As you rehearse and speak this new reality to yourself, life events begin to line up in favor of the change. You recognize these events because your new reality has written the memory of them in your brain. Your intuition, which is the sense of knowing a situation before it happens, will alert your awareness to come to attention. Using your will to choose God's thoughts resulted in a change of perspective. Your perception changed when what you imagined became normal for you in thought, feelings, conversation, and action.

You have a purpose and a path to follow that will fulfill the desires of your heart. God's good pleasure is to prosper you. To fulfill your purpose, use what you have learned to live and walk, led by the Holy Spirit, expecting to receive all that is necessary for success. Taking on the task of changing the whole world would be overwhelming for anyone but God. Knowing, with God, all things are possible, gives you faith and courage to learn and pursue the promises of God with diligence, for all the promises of God are yes and Amen in Jesus Christ. How to succeed by applying what you've learned is the beginning of living by faith. Once you begin to understand and apply the way of God to your daily life, you can receive the truth and live the victorious life God intended.

PART 2: THE PURPOSE

Chapter 4

Summary Questions

&

Reference Scriptures

PART 2: THE PURPOSE
Chapter 4 Summary Questions

Stepping Into Unlimited Possibilities
The Two-Way Open-Ended Lens

1. Have you experienced a 180 degree turn that revealed God's heart perspective, causing your perception to change?

2. Do you believe that God will work with you to change or heal any area of your life?

3. What have you trusted the right hand of God to accomplish for you or others?

4. Are you aware of the possibilities the death, burial, and resurrection of Jesus Christ has provided for you to obtain?

5. Do you consider yourself a citizen of heaven? If so, how do you view the various opportunities that already belong to you?

6. Name something you would like to change that you previously thought was unchangeable.

7. Give reasons why people experience difficulty seeing a progressive change in various areas of their lives.

8. Do you understand how to use your spirit and soul to receive from God?

9. Can you forcibly change how another person thinks?

10. What is your purpose?

Chapter 4 Scripture References
Descriptive Notes Taken from the Scripture for Research

Seated at His Right Hand

John 4:24
God is a Spirit.

Psalm 82:6
I have said, 'You are gods; and all of you are children of the most High.'

John 10:34
Jesus answered them, 'Is it not written in your law, I said, 'You are gods?'

Genesis 1:28
And God blessed them, and said, "Be fruitful, multiply, replenish the earth, subdue it: and have dominion."

Ephesians 2:4-8
God has quickened us together with Christ, raised us up together, and made us sit together in heavenly places in Christ Jesus.

Purpose as a Citizen of Heaven

Ephesians 1:9-12
We have obtained an inheritance, being predestinated according to the purpose of God. He works all things after the counsel of his own will.

II Peter 1:1-3
His divine power hath given unto us all things that pertain to life and godliness.

Ephesians 2:19-21
You are fellow citizens with the saints, of the household of God.

The Preeminence of the Lord Jesus Christ

Colossians 1:10-20
He is the head of the body, the church: who is the beginning, the firstborn from the dead; that in all things he might have the preeminence.

Be Imitators of God

Ephesians 5:1-2
Be imitators of God as dear children.

Genesis 1:1-5
And God called the light Day, and the darkness he called Night. And the evening and the morning were the first day.

All the Promises of God Are Yes and Amen

II Corinthians 1:19-20
In the Son of God, Jesus Christ, was yes. All the promises of God in him are yes, and in him Amen, unto the glory of God by us.

Controlled Environment - Blinded

I Corinthians 4:1-4
If our gospel is hid, it is hidden to them that are lost: In whom the god of this world hath blinded the minds of them which believe not.

Change What Others Believe Cannot Be Changed

Romans 4:18-22
Abraham was strong in faith. He was fully persuaded that, what God had promised, he was also able to perform.

Hebrews 11:3
Through faith, we understand that the worlds were framed by the word of God. So that those things which are seen were not made of things which do appear.

PART 3: THE PLAN

Transformation

CHAPTER 5

The Necessity of God's Plan
Infallible Assurance

Since his first step of freedom into the life, love, and light of God's presence, the unaware immature puppet boy who once represented the manipulation and control of other people, now has his eyes opened to a new perspective. With a simple 180 degree turn and lift to the fourth dimension, his perspective changed from a glimmer of light to God's heart perspective. No longer could oppression manipulate and mask his perception of the limitless possibilities heaven offered. His expanded knowledge and view of life's possibilities gave him a new sense of power on a grand scale. Possessing the freedom to choose and maneuver through unlimited versus limited possibilities, the boy realizes that freedom of choice requires the alignment of knowledge with the power of understanding, direction, and action. To evolve toward the fulfillment of his life's purpose, he decides to learn how to follow the lead of the Holy Spirit, who knows the deep things of God. The necessity of God's plan concerning his life's purpose would answer a crucial, 'Where is my life going, and how do I get there from here?'

Deciding to receive God's perfect plan is necessary to achieve success in any endeavor you undertake. Because God's kingdom rules over all, his plan must be infallible from beginning to end. He creates his plan, then speaks it into completion from his throne in the heavens. Because his view is from the completed result, the Word he speaks performs his desires. God's spoken Word increases in power and fruitfulness to accomplish his pleasure. It is carried out from start to finish in whatever and wherever he sends it.

How does God's Word increase in power and fruitfulness to accomplish his pleasure in your life? Begin by looking at the life of Jesus Christ. The atmosphere he maintained within and around himself was the realm of heaven on earth. His love, peace, joy, health, strength, wealth, wisdom, success, actions, etc., were in harmony with God's desires because he aligned himself with his Father in heaven through the power of the Holy Spirit. As Jesus said, 'I always do those things that pleased him.' He did not seek his own will but sought out the will of his Father who sent him. To experience spiritual increase, begin by deciding to learn and actively follow the Father's will by doing the things that please him.

Just as Jesus Christ followed the leading of the Holy Spirit and was predestined to pursue and finish his Father's plan for his life, you were uniquely made to live your best life in agreement with God's completed plan for you. Discover the power of living in one accord with your Father God, Jesus Christ, and the Holy Spirit. Remember, your life is hidden with Christ in God. Jesus prayed in John chapter 17, verses 20 through 24, for all those who believed in him at the time, and for those who would believe in him. The Father powerfully answered Jesus' prayer at his resurrection, his ascension, and in his sending the Holy Spirit to the earth. The glory of God raised Jesus Christ. He ascended in glory to the right hand of his Father, and then at Pentecost to believers who were of one mind in one place, he sent the Holy Spirit to fill them with power to be witnesses unto him in the world. Jesus Christ finished his Father's plan that the world may believe and know that the Father sent him and loved them as he loved him. His Father loved him before the foundation of the world.

Just as Jesus is one in the Father, and the Father is one in him, you are one in Jesus and the Father, with other believers. The glory of God is in believers, making them perfect in one in the Father and Jesus. He is your peace. How can this be? Now, created in Christ Jesus to do good works which God previously ordained for you, you have been made one with other believers by his Blood. He made himself of two, Israel and Gentile, one new man, and so making peace. Now, you can behold his glory in you and around you. To receive and access all that is available to you, act on it with one step of faith, believing in the love of God. Jesus Christ is one in God, and in him, so are you.

What does this mean for you? Right now, you are a citizen of heaven with the ability to speak your Father's will and live a lifestyle that has risen above the norm. When you realize, receive your inherited position with Jesus Christ at the right hand of the throne of God, and live your life from this perspective, your perception of life on earth changes. Through the power of the Holy Spirit and the Blood of Jesus, the power of God is available to you and increases in your life as you progressively align with who he is. Your thoughts, feelings, words, and actions are essential factors in discovering, learning, and living life to fulfillment.

Filled with and standing in the presence of God, you can learn to think as God thinks, feel as he feels, say what he says, and do what he shows you. Also standing there with Jesus Christ, the mediator of the New Covenant, and you, are an innumerable company of angels, and the cloud of witnesses. Knowing that God's plan is infallible, cautions you to receive his will, learn his thoughts and ways by listening for and applying his wisdom, knowledge, and understanding, then take action with 100 percent certainty of success. You can be confident that when God begins a good work in you, he will continue to perfect it until Jesus Christ returns from heaven. God working in you is not a one-way force that demands action on your part. He completes his will in your life with your cooperation. To work together with God is a privilege full of his love, power, presence, and grace.

Because you now have the mind of Christ, renewing your mind to understand how to live from the spiritual realm is vital. God's way of living from the heavenly realm to the earth realm for you, is by faith, hope, and love. He is the God of hope. Developing the gospel of God in you enables his power to change, replenish, rearrange, heal, and manifest his goodness, etc. in various areas of your life. Knowing how to live by the faith of Jesus Christ in you is necessary to complete the unique plan God has for you. Renewing your mind by receiving the knowledge that the gospel of Christ is the power of God, begins to build his faith in you. Believing then acting on the good news of the gospel, that you are joint-heirs with Jesus Christ, is to receive the things God created in heaven as complete and real. God tells you what he desires for you to believe for, or as you learn from him, you develop the ability also to decide what to manifest for yourself or others. Initiating the process and action of faith allows these things to enter your life from the heavenly realm. By the power of the Holy Spirit that is working in you, God is more than able to carry out his purpose through you. He does exceeding abundantly above and infinitely beyond all that you can think, ask, or dream.

You know that God is love. What are hope and faith? How do you develop hope and the confidence to believe that God will answer your prayers? Hope is the expectation of good. Developing hope is developing trust in God's love. Since God is love, then love is all-powerful. Nothing can move God out of himself, so no power can stop your requests from effecting your life unless you intervene with doubt and unbelief. Is God 100 percent for you or 100 percent against you? A simple answer to this question is the truth of the death, burial, and resurrection of his Son Jesus Christ. There is no way you can enjoy God's love, grace, mercy and the goodness of God unless you realize that his sending his Son to redeem you from the power of eternal death and the grave was because he loves you. Jesus Christ finished his Father's plan on earth and in heaven because of his love for his Father and you. God chose you. There is no good thing he will withhold from you because, in the Lord Jesus Christ, it has already been provided and belongs to you. The only question is, how do you transfer your desire from the spiritual realm to the natural realm? The answer, as found in Romans chapter 1, verse 17, is, the just shall live by faith.

The just are those whose way of thinking, feeling, and acting conforms to the will of God. Living in agreement with the intention of God means that God gives 100 percent to and for you, so you are to live your life 100 percent to and for him. Only by the grace and mercy of God in Jesus Christ can this be accomplished. Peace on earth, good will toward men, was restored by Jesus Christ. There is no doubt and unbelief or anything else negative in God's peace. Because Jesus was resurrected from death, hell, and the grave, he was given all power over anything you can ask or think of to believe and receive from God. Why wouldn't you trust the love of God for you and step into the end result with 100 percent assurance? Before his resurrection, living in the righteousness of God was not possible. Now your life is hidden with Christ Jesus in God, and to you, he is your wisdom, righteousness, sanctification, and redemption. To live by your way and what you think is right places you back in the thoughts, feelings, and actions of the crowd and not living the lifestyle of heaven. You have risen with Christ. Set your affection on things above where Christ sits on the right hand of God, and not on things on the earth.

How is the faith of Jesus Christ developed, and at work in you? Hebrews chapter 11, verse 1, says, now faith is the substance of things hoped for, the evidence of things not seen. What does this mean? The heavenly realm is not linear, like living on earth. In the spiritual realm, there is no time. What you call the past, present, and future are happening simultaneously on various spheres or realms in heaven. Now faith, which is the substance of the thing hoped for, works in the present tense. It's never too late or too soon.

The substance of the thing is formed in your spirit and soul. The spiritual realm is a reality where unlimited possibilities already exist. Realize that your spirit is one with the kingdom of heaven, and you presently live in and from the spiritual realm. God may show you a specific thing he desires to manifest through you, or you can decide what you would like to manifest in line with heaven's possibilities. First, know the purpose of what you want by describing its characteristics. Writing down what you specifically desire is also an excellent idea. Before you can hope for something, you have to know what you want and use your description to see its completion with clarity. Writing your list and speaking it out loud at least once a day, brings the spiritual realm into the natural. The list provides you with a written vision that helps you discern counterfeits and stay on course. Believing that you already have what you desire enables you to develop hope with feelings of joy and assurance.

How will you know the moment you believe and receive what you ask or think in the spiritual realm? Part of the process used to develop the substance of faith is the action of high hopes. The moment you believe you have received what you desire, God fills you with joy and peace that you may increase in hope through the power of the Holy Spirit. From this moment on, you possess the certainty that you have what you asked. An example of this process is found in Genesis chapter 1, verses 1 through 5. God created the heaven and the earth. The earth had no form and was empty. God used his imagination to see the completion of his work before he called light out of the darkness. The Holy Spirit moved upon the surface of the waters, preparing it to receive his commands. At God's command, 'Let there be light,' light appeared. He saw that the light was good and then divided it from the darkness. Always creating with purpose, God called the light Day and the darkness, Night.

Continue to maintain high expectations for what you desire regardless of negative words, emotions, circumstances, or unexpected events. In your imagination, you can go anywhere, be anyone, do, and have anything. The action of hoping is exercising your thoughts with feelings of joyful expectation by using your imagination to create. The Holy Spirit helps you form and imagine moving, colorful, video clips filled with spoken words, godly emotions, and actions celebrating your joyful result. Whatever or whoever you are amassing substance for takes the leading role. Imagine the scenes in reality from within the scene, not looking towards yourself in the moving scene as a spectator. There is no opposition in the heavenly realm. As long as you use your imagination with the highest levels of love, confident expectation, and feelings of joy, you create faith substance of the thing you desire. Faith, which works by love, sustains your confidence in God that you have what you requested. Faith substance is the evidence in your spirit that you have what you desire now.

Allow the godly forces of hope, faith, and love from the point of rest to work for you. Concerning yourself with how it will happen, removes you from the end result and places you at the beginning or with the persistent problem, and no solution. Placing yourself within the result by celebrating it now allows God to work on your behalf. He uses his presence, knowledge, and power to perform what is necessary according to the power at work in you between 'I believe I have it now' and 'thank you, what I desired has happened in my life.'

The following is an experience of faith the Holy Spirit used to teach me how to manifest what God desired for me. As you will see, you work with God because, with God, all things are possible.

How God Sold My House in a Failing Market

The housing market in California was declining fast in 2005. I owned a home built in the 1950s in an area that was known for crime and gangs. People were not rushing there to purchase any property. My neighborhood, because we lived there, was protected by God. At times, on the weekends, we would hear police helicopters and gunfire, but no matter what went on around us, God would not allow it to touch our home or family. We were blessed, and our home and property were blessed.

In April of that year, the Holy Spirit told me, 'Fix up the house to sell it.' He had sent a message to me through a girlfriend of mine a few years earlier that I would get married again. I had been standing in faith on that word since then, with the help of manifestations and specific signs from the Holy Spirit that encouraged me. When he told me to fix up the house to sell it, I knew that the wedding was close and that I would soon find out who the blessed man would be. Ha, ha! Years earlier, I had asked the Holy Spirit to let me know for sure who the person was. I was determined to wait until I heard from the Holy Spirit and not to make another mistake by giving up and choosing someone on my own.

I asked my younger brother to help me find a handyman to work on the house. Certain things had to be brought up to code for the house to pass inspection. As I was driving home from church on the following Wednesday evening, I asked the Holy Spirit to give me the selling price. Sitting out in front of me through the windshield in the spirit as I drove, I was shown two 6-figure amounts at the same time. The first one was large, very clear, and close to me. The second amount was off in the distance and not so distinct. It was $10,000.00 less than the first figure. I knew that I was to list the house with the first amount and then, after a time, change the asking price to the second amount. Somehow I knew that the house would sell for the second amount.

As I expected, since I was told to fix up the house, within two months, the Holy Spirit let me know who God had chosen to be my husband. He lived in Texas. I had never been to Texas, nor had I ever thought about going there, but God always knows best. Through a series of glorious Holy Spirit manifestations, we were married in my church two weeks later. My new husband and I listed the house in September for the first price, the Holy Spirit showed me. People came, looked, and left with little interest. The realtor we had at the time did not believe the house would sell. The holiday season came and went. We changed realtors and lowered the list price for the home to the second figure the Holy Spirit showed me. Some of my friends tried to get me to rent the house instead of selling it, but without hesitation, I told them what God had said, 'Fix up the house to sell it.' Time passed, but I was not concerned about it. I knew that the Holy Spirit would let us know if there was anything more for us to do.

One day in the middle of March, a thought came to me that caused me to think forward. Since God told me to sell the house, then the home is sold. Then I asked myself, 'After the house sells, what would be our next step? We would go to Texas!' Continuing to ride this train of forward-thinking, out-loud I asked the Holy Spirit, "When will we leave for Texas?" With no hesitation, he said, 'the middle of April.' Well, since we had a 30-day escrow in place; that meant the buyers were coming the same week. It was Tuesday, so I asked the Holy Spirit what day the buyers were coming? He said, 'Thursday afternoon.' Knowing the buyers were coming was a relief to my husband because we had been paying the mortgages and expenses on two homes since our marriage. On Thursday morning, we received a call from the realtor. He would be bringing some people to see the house that afternoon. Even though there seemed to be problems with the people qualifying for the loan, we had no concerns about it because the Holy Spirit said that we would leave for Texas in the middle of April.

The sale of the house went through as scheduled, and we received the second 6-figure amount just as the Holy Spirit showed me through the windshield that night. Praise God! We left for Texas in the middle of April, just as the Holy Spirit said. Soon and I mean, very shortly after the sale of the house, the bottom fell out of the housing market. God knows the times and seasons of a person's life. He is good, and he is good to those who obey his word.

PART 3: THE PLAN

Chapter 5

Summary Questions
&
Reference Scriptures

PART 3: THE PLAN
Chapter 5 Summary Questions

The Necessity of God's Plan
Infallible Assurance

1. If you turned one thing in your life 180 degrees, how would it change your perspective?

2. Have you decided to ask for and receive God's plan for your life?

3. How does God's spoken Word increase in power and fruitfulness to accomplish his pleasure?

4. What is God's will? How do you know you are aligning yourself with his will?

5. Do you understand how and why you are one with God, the Lord Jesus Christ, and other believers?

6. You are a citizen of heaven right now. How does this change your perspective, perception, and thinking?

7. What does the statement, 'the just shall live by faith' mean to you?

8. Do you understand how substance forms faith according to Hebrews 11, verse 1?

9. How do faith, hope, and love work together in Jesus Christ?

10. How will you know the moment you believe and receive what you ask or think in the spiritual realm?

Chapter 5 Scripture References
Descriptive Notes Taken from the Scripture for Research

Why Should You Live by God's Plan?

Psalm 103:19
The LORD has prepared his throne in the heavens.

Psalm 16:11
You will shew me the path of life: in your presence is fullness of joy.

Isaiah 55:8-11
My word shall accomplish that which I please, and it shall prosper in the thing whereto I sent it.

The Father and I Are One

John 10:30
I and my Father are one.

John 17:20-24
That they all may be one; as you, Father, are in me, and I in you, that they also may be one in us.

Jesus Finished His Father's Plan

John 17:4
I have glorified you on the earth: I have finished the work which you gave me to do.

Ephesians 2:10-15
For he is our peace, who has made both one.

Hebrews 12:22-24
But you are come unto mount Sion, and unto the city of the living God, to Jesus, the mediator of the new covenant.

A Good Work in You

Philippians 1:6
He which has begun a good work in you will perform it until the day of Jesus Christ.

Renew Your Mind

I Corinthians 2:12-16
We have the mind of Christ.

Romans 12:2
And be not conformed to this world: but be transformed by the renewing of your mind.

Ephesians 4:22-24
And be renewed in the spirit of your mind.

No Good Thing Is Withheld

Psalm 84:11
No good thing will he withhold from them that walk uprightly.

Live by Faith

Romans 1:16-17
The gospel of Christ is the power of God unto salvation. The just shall live by faith.

Galatians 5:5-6
Faith works by love.

Hebrews 11:1
Now faith is the substance of things hoped for, the evidence of things not seen.

The Moment You Believe

Romans 15:13
The God of hope fills you with all joy and peace in believing.

Ephesians 3:14-21
Now unto him that is able to do exceeding abundantly above all that we ask or think.

Genesis 1:1-5
The Spirit of God moved upon the face of the waters. Let there be light: and there was light.

CHAPTER 6

The Power of Restful Transformation

Inherent Power

The boy puppet has decided to live a faith-filled life of purpose, wholly following the Spirit of God. He has been standing in his presence, listening, and learning. Even though what he learned has changed his perspective and perception of life, his questions remain. 'Where is my life going, and how do I get there from here?' Knowing his thoughts, God asks, "Where would you like to go?" The boy replies, "I'm not sure. It's so exciting! I don't know which way to go or what to choose first. I've been standing here for a while, listening, looking, and learning. All around me, I see unlimited possibilities of places to go and all sorts of things I can do and have. How will I know I can do all these things? I'm just a puppet." "No," God stops him, "you are no longer a puppet.

You're free. You are alive in me! Look! See what I see. You can think and choose and move. Yes, and now you can walk."

The boy takes a step, then two steps, and then four quick steps. "I can walk on my own!" he exclaims. He lifts his head, then closes his eyes. With a sigh of grateful relief, he opens them again. Thinking of remaining free while facing his former opposition, he takes a deep breath, then slowly exhales. Thoughtfully he asks, "I'm free, but am I strong enough to make the right choices, step into your plan and carry out my purpose? God empowers him. "Receive the gift of the Holy Spirit. Know that his power indwells you at all times. The strength and power of my knowledge with wisdom and understanding will guide you to fulfill your purpose. Resting in me is key to receiving in your spirit."

Even though his oppressor was no longer present, the effects of deep pain, hurt feelings, and lack of knowledge, confidence, and direction remained. Now, to follow God's plan for his life, the boy must be taught and led by the Holy Spirit and not by the outside forces of oppression that once controlled him. Because everything is changing in his life from the inside out, he must know that his abilities are encouraged and developed by God's hand and not regulated by his former oppressor.

Before you can have dominion in the earth, you must allow the Holy Spirit's authority over your spirit, soul, and body. In the same manner, as you show loving respect for a parent, ask for, and receive the baptism in the Holy Spirit. Expect to receive the gifts of the Holy Spirit, including the ability to pray in tongues. Relax, take a breath and speak the sound you see or hear, even if it's one syllable. As you pray in tongues, the Holy Spirit begins to pray through you. Submit to him, allowing his ability to join yours in prayer. Praying in tongues, your heavenly language, is yours to develop in private between you and God. Continue to practice speaking the sound or sounds until you become comfortable with your new language. Practicing develops your tongues from 'baby talk' to adult ability. You may think that because you only received one or two syllables, that when you speak in tongues, they are not very powerful. This gift is from the Holy Spirit, and nothing about him is weak.

Your heavenly language benefits you, not others who would not know what you are saying. If you are in a setting where people expect the gift of interpretation of tongues, then your heavenly language, or the gift of tongues intended for that particular time, would be of benefit to others. You can ask for the interpretation, or someone else can ask and receive it to teach or instruct others. If information about a person's sickness, or an urgent situation is at hand, ask the Holy Spirit for a solution, then pray in tongues and listen for the answer. He will show you the answer by various means, or you will hear what to do. Whichever means he uses, say it, or do what you see in Jesus' name.

To maintain control of the former thoughts and ways of the old man in spirit, soul, and body, begin by exercising your sense of awareness and discernment. The old man in you is spiritually dead, but his ways of thinking, speaking, and acting will still try to manipulate your life. Stay aware of his ways by using them to discern the difference between living your life in freedom, or 'living' in oppression. Resting in eternal life, love, and light is trusting in who God is, and his ability over yours. Entering into spiritual rest begins by giving up your previous experience for his, your idea of love for his unconditional love, and from following the crowd to receiving and releasing revelation and power from the Holy Spirit, who is in you.

In Genesis chapter 1, verse 28, God blessed you and said, "Be fruitful, multiply, replenish the earth, subdue it, and have dominion." Adam did not resist when God put him in the Garden of Eden. Jesus, after his baptism, did not resist being led by the Holy Spirit to fast and be tempted by the devil in the wilderness. Adam lived in perfection. He possessed all he needed to protect his atmosphere, environment, and surroundings. Although Jesus lived in a world system controlled by the enemy, he was not controlled by him. Jesus lived in the world system, but nothing about his life was effect by that world system because he represented the kingdom of heaven everywhere he traveled. Forty days of fasting increased his power and enhanced the clarity of his spiritual senses, allowing him to boldly release the Word of God in wisdom, knowledge, and power, to counter the devil's distortion of the Word. Not able to overcome Jesus in the wilderness by tempting him with the very things he created, the enemy, defeated, left him until another time. After the angels ministered to him, he returned in power to Galilee, announced, and began his ministry, saying, "Repent, for the kingdom of heaven is at hand."

Be fruitful, by multiplying, and replenishing the fruit of the Spirit, which describes the character and inherent power of God. Fully developed, the fruit is mature in form and strength. God is love. There is no law against God, so there is no law against producing, bearing, or growing his fruit. All nine characteristics displaying the inherent power of God's love, emanate from and are always in action and on constant display from God himself. They are love, joy, peace, longsuffering, gentleness, goodness, faithfulness, meekness, and temperance. The power of the Holy Spirit flows unhindered through Jesus Christ in his compassion for others because he rests 100 percent in his Father. He is your example of being led by the Spirit and powerfully manifesting the flow of his power without hindrance from his spirit, soul, or body.

Transformation in God's rest was evident in Jesus' life because he lived a powerfully spirit controlled life on earth. Although Jesus was equal with God, he humbled himself, took on the form of a servant, and was born, made in the likeness of men. From childhood, he grew strong in spirit and filled with God's wisdom. The following are some examples of spiritual fruit produced in his life and ministry. Governed by the divine power of grace, he was kept, strengthened, and increased in faith, knowledge, and love. Anointed by his Father with the Holy Spirit and with power, the expectation of his goodness proceeded him. God was with him as he went about doing good and healing all that the devil oppressed. As the Father loves him, he loves you. In the Garden of Gethsemane, after Judas and the multitude came to take him away, one of his disciples struck Malchus, the servant of the high priest, and cut off his ear. Displaying gentleness, Jesus touched his ear and healed him. Showing self-control, Jesus said, 'Do you think that I cannot now pray to my Father, and he shall presently give me more than twelve legions of angels? But how then shall the scriptures be fulfilled, that this is how it must be?'

He manifested God's love throughout his ministry and by his sacrifice on the cross of Calvary for all humankind. He became obedient to death on the cross. Look to Jesus as the beginner and the finisher of your faith. He received the strength of joy from his Father to endure the cross because he saw himself at his right hand. Although the disciples were sorrowful at his departure, he left his never-ending peace with them and told them that when he saw them again, their hearts would rejoice. No man could take their joy from them, and no one can take your joy from you. Jesus Christ showed Apostle Paul mercy and all longsuffering for a pattern to those who would afterward believe on him to life everlasting.

For you, being aligned in love with the perfect will of God is a powerful thing. Love never fails. Living by faith, which works by love, is showing faithfulness by believing God in all things. Finding the strength of joy deep within, even in sorrow, is knowing how to rejoice in the truth. Jesus Christ is the Prince of Peace in you. To have Jesus Christ in your heart is to have peace no matter what life brings. The strength of patience is the long-suffering of love. Love is gentle and kind. To love is to show gentleness and kindness in the face of adversity or difficulty. Love hopes all things and endures all things. The God of hope fills you with all joy and peace when you believe so that you may choose to abound in hope through the Holy Spirit. To hope is to use your belief, feelings, and imagination to create the substance of love's goodness. Meekness and temperance work together in love. Humility is meekness in action as controlled spiritual strength. Temperance is displaying self-control by monitoring your feelings and controlling your actions.

From the position of rest, your transformation by the power of the Holy Spirit gives you further understanding of the Lord's kingdom. You have received a kingdom that cannot be shaken. The increase of his government and peace never ends. Where his Spirit is, you have freedom. To receive, develop, grow, and transform spiritually in freedom, focus on eternal life, love, and light in his realm. The faith, strength, and power of the Holy Spirit he lived by and displayed on earth, was received from his Father because he rested in him. He lived his life by trusting in his Father's strength 100 percent, and not on his ability. Becoming gentle and humble in heart like Jesus makes his yoke easy for you to carry, and your burden of light to change the world system is released from rest. To find rest for your soul, take his raised yoke, and use it to learn from him.

The Holy Spirit leads you as you walk in one accord with him. Called to walk in freedom, you can hear his voice more clearly from the spiritual and mental rest Christ provided for you. Exercising your dominion to express and grow the fruit of the Spirit denies access to your old way of controlled living. Learning to love the Father with all your heart, soul, mind, and strength as Jesus does, is not something you can do on your own. Your body is now the temple of the Holy Spirit, who teaches you how to live a fruit-producing life of faith in Jesus Christ. You cannot bear fruit alone. Only by remaining in him, can you glorify the Father by bringing forth an abundance of fruit. Continue in his love. The Holy Spirit reveals God's righteousness in you from one level of trust to the next. By faith, he increases your ability to believe the Word. Knowing God's in-depth desires for you, the Holy Spirit shows you how to grow and release faith in and around your unique God-given plan. He knows the deep things of God and the deep things of your heart. Using the thoughts of your heart, he teaches you and then shows you how to align your desires with your Father in heaven.

The result of aligning with God's desires is that you will love others as you love yourself. The Holy Spirit knows what is best for you by comparing the spiritual things of God with the spiritual elements in your heart, good or bad. He then presents choices, whether they are spiritual, mental, physical, or situational. Using the choices you make, he teaches you God's thoughts and ways. Some decisions can be tough to make when negatively charged emotions arise amid life's difficult situations. Emotional pictures begin to flood your mind, and the feelings that ensue will try to pressure you into solving the problem yourself. Do not forge ahead, doing what you think is best. Allowing the Holy Spirit to speak to you will avoid the spiritual hindrances that negative thoughts and emotions create, trying to stifle your progress.

At this time of pressured indecision, consider asking the Holy Spirit for wisdom and understanding from a state of rest. Exploring on your own is not an option if you desire to know and progress in life by the deep things of God. You can use your free will to live life wanting your way, or you can choose to live your best life by following the Holy Spirit's lead. How do you rest in alignment with God's desires? His Word is his desire. Because God is eternal life, he does not speak anything he does not desire to take place. His Word is alive and powerful. A two-edged sword is one that cuts going and coming. When you align with and speak his Word in faith, you release the eternal life and power in his spoken Word that he has already released to completion. The Word pierces and divides the soul from the spirit. You have been reborn. Your spirit is brand new, and one with the Spirit of God, but your soul needs work to believe and receive the things of God. Your soul at rest is the turnstile that allows access from the Holy Spirit to your spirit. As the elements of your soul, the mind, will, emotions, intellect, and imagination transform by the will of God, changes manifest in your body and the circumstances of your life. The Word also discerns the thoughts and intents of your heart. Your heart and soul work together by using the faculties of the mind, which include reason, memory, intuition, and perception.

Using what you've learned about entering into God's rest, combine it with the knowledge of God and your Savior Jesus Christ to manifest his precious promises. Multiplied to you through the knowledge of God and Jesus Christ, are his grace and peace. His divine power has given you everything you will ever need for your life and to show reverence towards God. All of these things are yours and are available to you now through the knowledge of God. What do you need to know to manifest these precious promises?

The following definitions of some essential words in II Peter chapter 1, verses 1 through 4, will be used to explain more clearly how to manifest the precious promises of God. These promises are manifest from the position of rest.

- Grace is the divine influence upon your heart, and its reflection in your life, including gratitude, joy, pleasure, delight, and sweetness.

- Peace is harmony, concord, security, safety, prosperity, tranquil state of the soul assured of its salvation through Jesus Christ, quietness, rest, and set at one again.

- Divine Power is the strength, ability, inherent power residing in a thing by virtue of its nature, power for performing miracles, and moral power and excellence of soul.

- Knowledge of God and Jesus, our Lord is full discernment, precise and correct knowledge, and knowledge of things ethical and divine.

- Glory is dignity, honor, praise, worship, opinion, judgment, and view. God's opinion is always good, resulting in praise, honor, and glory. It is magnificence, excellence, preeminence, and majesty. Glory is the absolutely perfect inward or personal excellency of Christ, which is the majesty and glorious condition of blessedness.

- Virtue is an excellent course of thought, feeling, and action. It is moral goodness and any particular moral excellence as modesty and purity.

- Divine Nature is the nature of things, the force, laws, and order of nature. It is a mode of feeling and acting which by long habit has become life. It is the sum of inherent properties and powers by which one person differs from others, distinctive native peculiarities, and natural characteristics.

A clear explanation of God's divine power and nature inherent in you enables you to manifest your precious promises now. Verses 4 through 8 of II Peter chapter 1, are a road map where you use the inherent power of your restful transformation. Verses 1 through 4 informs you of the Divine in you. Receiving, focusing, and then releasing the divine power of God is living eternal life now, after the resurrection of Jesus Christ.

Giving all diligence, earnestly add to your faith, which is the conviction of the truth of anything, belief, and trust, virtue. Virtue engages your thoughts, feelings, and actions. Collective thoughts develop imaginary living scenes, seen and experienced with feelings that lead to actions creating the substance of faith. Add to your faith, virtue, and virtue knowledge. Faith sees, feels, and lives from the things hoped for with love and gratitude. Using virtue to develop faith does you no good without knowing the details and purpose of what you have created. Knowledge is general intelligence and understanding. Add self-control, which is temperance to knowledge. Living in the spiritual realm with focused virtue that creates the substance called faith, without self-control, once the knowledge of its purpose is known, will lead to misuse and waste. To temperance, add patience, which is endurance. Once you have believed, used your senses, and received in the spiritual realm what already belongs to you, patience is necessary to see it through to manifestation. From a soul at rest, you can hear the voice of the Holy Spirit and follow his instructions to manifest from the heavenly realm to the earthly realm.

Adding godliness to patience is living in reverence and respect for God and his promises. Then brotherly kindness toward one another is added to godliness, and brotherly love, which is your affection, good will, and benevolence, is added to brotherly kindness. To develop, and partake of the divine nature through the knowledge of Jesus Christ in you, is partnering with the Divine to manifest your precious promises. When all of these things, faith, virtue, knowledge, temperance, patience, godliness, brotherly kindness, and brotherly love are in you and increase, you will neither be idle nor unfruitful in the knowledge of the Lord Jesus Christ.

Because Jesus learned to live with his soul at rest, the Spirit of the LORD could rest on him, revealing the spirit of wisdom, understanding, counsel, might, knowledge and the fear of the LORD. Jesus lived a life of reverence for his Father. By revelation from the Holy Spirit, he fulfilled his course of life and ministry by his Father's divine power and nature. What is the fear or reverence of the Lord? The answer is found in Psalm Chapter 34, verses 11 through 14. Come, you children, listen to me and understand. I will teach you the fear of the LORD. What man is he that desires life, and loves many days, that he may see good things such as benefit, welfare, prosperity, happiness, wealth, and favor? Keep your tongue from evil, and your mouth from speaking deceit and betrayal. Depart from evil, and do good; seek peace, and pursue it. Good fruit or bad fruit is also a product of the tongue after you have formed it in your spirit. Proverbs chapter 18, verses 20 and 21 say a man's belly shall be satisfied with the fruit of his mouth; and with the increase of his lips shall he be filled. Death and life are in the power of the tongue: and they that love it shall eat the fruit thereof. The fruit is good or bad, sweet or rotten, green or ripe. After you have lived your life in the reality of the spiritual realm, live what you have created in the natural realm by allowing the Holy Spirit to direct you from your soul at rest.

PART 3: THE PLAN

Chapter 6

Summary Questions
&
Reference Scriptures

PART 3: THE PLAN
Chapter 6 Summary Questions

The Power of Restful Transformation
Inherent Power

1. Do you understand the difference between when to pray using your heavenly language and the gift of tongues?
2. What makes your soul the turnstile from your spirit to your body?
3. Why is resting in God key to receiving in your spirit?
4. Why should you focus on eternal life, love, and light in the kingdom?
5. Do you understand why inherent power emanates from spiritual rest?
6. How was restful transformation evident in the life of Jesus?
7. Does 100 percent mean loving God with all your heart, soul, mind, and strength?
8. When you live your life wholly by the Spirit of God, what can you expect?
9. The precious promises of God are available to you through the knowledge of God and Jesus Christ our Savior. How do you manifest them in your life?
10. Accessing and releasing the revelatory power of God through the Holy Spirit is to give glory to God. What is the reverential fear of the Lord?

Chapter 6 Scripture References
Descriptive Notes Taken from the Scripture for Research

Receive the Holy Spirit

Luke 11:13
The Father gives the Holy Spirit to those who ask.

Acts 1:8
You shall receive power, after that the Holy Ghost comes upon you.

Jude 1:20-21
But you, beloved, building up yourselves on your most holy faith, praying in the Holy Ghost.

Acts 8:14-17
They laid their hands on them, and they received the Holy Ghost.

Praying in Tongues

I Corinthians 12:4-11
The manifestation of the Spirit is given to every man to profit with; different kinds of tongues, the interpretation of tongues.

I Corinthians 14:14-19
I thank my God, I speak with tongues more than you all. Yet in the church I had rather speak five words with my understanding.

Jude 1:20-21
Building up yourselves on your most holy faith, praying in the Holy Ghost.

Maintain Control of Your Former Thoughts

Hebrews 5:13-14
People of full age are those who have exercised their senses to discern both good and evil.

Ephesians 4:22-24
Put off the old man. Put on the new man, which is created after God in righteousness and true holiness.

Colossians 3:9-10
Put on the new man, which is renewed in knowledge after the image of him that created him.

Rest in God: The Key to Being Fruitful

I Corinthians 2:12-13
Know the things God freely gives us.

Genesis 1:28
God blessed them and said, "Be fruitful, multiply, replenish the earth, and subdue it. Have dominion."

Be Led by the Spirit with No Resistance

Genesis 2:8
The LORD God planted a garden eastward in Eden and put the man there.

Luke 4:1-2
Jesus being full of the Holy Ghost, was led by the Spirit into the wilderness.

Galatians 5:18, 25
Be led by the Spirit. Live and walk in the Spirit.

My Kingdom and I Are Not of This World

Matthew 3:2
Repent, for the kingdom of heaven is at hand.

John 18:36
My kingdom is not of this world.

John 8:23
You are of this world; I am not of this world.

John 17:14-16
They are not of this world, even as I am of this world.

Manifest the Fruit of the Spirit

Galatians 5:22-23
The fruit of the Spirit is love, joy, peace, longsuffering, gentleness, goodness, faith, meekness, temperance: against such there is no law.

Colossians 1:9-11
Be filled with the knowledge of his will in all wisdom and spiritual understanding. Be fruitful in every good work.

Colossians 3:12-15
Put on bowels of mercies, kindness, humbleness of mind, meekness, longsuffering. Forgive. Above all these things put on love and let the peace of God rule in your hearts.

I Corinthians 13:4-8, 13
Love never fails. Faith, hope, and love remain. The greatest of these is love.

John 15:16
I have chosen you, and ordained you, that you should go and bring forth fruit, and that your fruit should remain.

John 15:17
My commandment, that you love one another, as I have loved you.

The Kingdom of the Lord Jesus Christ

Hebrews 12:28-29
Wherefore we receiving a kingdom which cannot be moved, let us serve God acceptably with reverence and godly fear.

Isaiah 9:7
The increase of his government and peace never ends.

II Corinthians 3:17-18
Now the Lord is that Spirit: and where the Spirit of the Lord is, there is freedom.

Romans 14:17
The kingdom of God is righteousness, peace, and joy in the Holy Ghost.

Matthew 11:28-30
Come to me, all you that labor and are heavy laden, and I will give you rest. My yoke is easy, and my burden is light.

Hebrews 4:8-11
There remains, therefore, a rest to the people of God. He that enters into his rest has ceased from his works, as God did from his.

Called to Freedom, Your Body is the Temple of the Holy Ghost

Galatians 5:13-16
You are called freedom. By love, serve one another.

Mark 12:30-31
Love the Lord your God with all your heart, soul, mind, and strength. Love your neighbor as yourself.

Psalm 111:1
I will praise the LORD with my whole heart.

I Corinthians 6:19-20
Do you know that your body is the temple of the Holy Ghost which is in you, which you have of God, and you are not your own?

John 15:1-5
Abide in me, and I in you. He that abides in me, and I in him, the same brings forth much fruit, for without me you can do nothing.

The Holy Spirit Teaches You

I Corinthians 2:13
The wisdom the Holy Ghost teaches; comparing spiritual things with spiritual.

II Corinthians 4:16
Though our outward man perishes, yet the inward man is renewed day by day.

John 16:13-15
When the Spirit of truth comes, he will guide you into all truth, and he will shew you things to come.

Renew Your Mind

Romans 12:2
Be not conformed to this world, but be transformed by the renewing of your mind.

Romans 8:6
For to be carnally minded is death, but to be spiritually minded is life and peace.

Ephesians 4:23
Be renewed in the spirit of your mind.

Hebrews 4:12
The word of God is quick, and powerful, and sharper than any two-edged sword, and is a discerner of the thoughts and intents of the heart.

Philippians 4:7
The peace of God, which passes all understanding, shall keep your hearts and minds through Christ Jesus.

Your Spiritual Map

Colossians 1:12
The Father has made us able to partake of the inheritance of the saints in light.

II Peter 1:1-11
Grace and peace multiply to you through the knowledge of God, and Jesus our Lord.

A Soul at Rest in the Fear of the Lord

Isaiah 11:1-2
The Spirit of the Lord could rest on him, revealing the spirit of wisdom, understanding, counsel, might, knowledge, and the fear of the Lord.

Isaiah 11:3
The Spirit shall make him of quick understanding in the fear of the LORD.

Proverbs 9:10-11
The fear of the LORD is the beginning of wisdom: and the knowledge of the holy is understanding.

Psalm 111:10
The fear of the LORD is the beginning of wisdom.

Psalm 34:11-14
Come, you children, hearken unto me: I will teach you the fear of the LORD.

Proverbs 18:20-21
A man's belly shall be satisfied with the fruit of his mouth. Death and life are in the power of the tongue.

CHAPTER 7

Increase in Spiritual Strength and Power

Close Doors to Negative Thoughts, Words, and Actions

•

The boy, no longer a puppet, is filled with the power of the Holy Spirit and learning how to remain free as he lives his new life. The Holy Spirit rested on him, teaching him to develop fruit, and by God's divine nature, obtain his God-given promises through divine knowledge. Learning from God, in the realm of heaven, is two-sided. Through the two-way open-ended lens, the boy has seen the unlimited possibilities of heaven versus the changeable limitations on earth. He knows that whatever choice he makes, it's either sanctioned by the realm of heaven or the realm of the earth. To choose God's way and his plan is to choose life and blessing.

Before he can develop his senses, maintain spiritual strength, and be effectively led by the Holy Spirit in adversity, the boy's next lesson is to learn how to forgive. Closing the doors to negative thoughts, words, and actions by forgiving will allow him to access, maintain, and increase in spiritual strength and power. God informs him, "Before you can move forward, you must open your heart, expand your thinking, and receive healing for your soul. You cannot fulfill my plan for your course of life by living from your emotions, but by my spirit." The boy thinks for a brief moment and then responds. "I'm ready to do what I have to do to move forward." He was well aware of his helplessness under the control of the puppet master, who once possessed the ability to maneuver his every move skillfully. Remembering his inability to see, hear, think, speak, move, or do anything for himself, he boldly declares, "I will not let the puppet master possess my ability ever again! I am who I am now because I live and walk in you, Father."

Forgiveness begins by choosing to give up your hurt, pain, disappointment, injustice, etc. for joy, peace, and healing in God's presence surrounded by the power of his unconditional love. Reliving negative memories by recounting and reacting to familiar sounds, spoken words, feelings, and actions, keeps them close to you. Every time you entertain negativity, allowing visual reenactments filled with conversations, painful emotions, etc., it grows spiritually and increases in strength. You make yourself a prey for those who would seek to control you by remaining in the same condition. The original condition of the young boy shows us the importance of why you must forgive yourself and others.

Knowing you must forgive is one thing, but agreeing to forgive and having the strength to forgive sincerely is another. Once you have decided to forgive someone or yourself, the battle of emotions and hurt feelings versus forgiveness begins. Decide to love your enemies and forgive. Make love and forgiveness a priority to remain free and clear of doubt and unbelief so you can hear the Holy Spirit's voice at any moment. The intensity of each outcome is determined by who or what you agree with at the moment. Paying attention to your thoughts, feelings, words, and actions give you a reading on negative versus positive, monitored, and gauged by your unforgiveness or forgiveness.

From the cross, Jesus interceded for the ones who crucified him. He asked his Father to forgive them. God, who is unconditional love, forgave them. Jesus did not forgive them from the cross because unforgiveness is a sin, and he refused to enter hell without it. Unforgiveness is just one sin. He removed all resistance to his enemy, Satan, and allowed his soul to travail in hell for all sin. One prophecy of his planned death and resurrection is found in Isaiah 53, verses 1 through 12. Verse 10 tells us that it pleased the LORD to bruise him. He had put him to grief. When he shall make his soul an offering for sin, he shall see his seed and prolong his days. The pleasure of the LORD shall prosper in his hand. After paying for our sin, Jesus, without the resistance to his Father, was raised by the glory of the Father.

After his resurrection, Jesus Christ ascended to the right hand of his Father. He is the head of the body, which is composed of all Christ-like people, called the church. He is the beginning, the firstborn from the dead, that in all things, he will occupy the first place standing supreme and preeminent. It pleased the Father that in him all fullness of deity, the sum total of his essence, all his perfection, powers, and attributes permanently dwell. Forgiving from the heart connects you powerfully to the power of the Father, his Son, and the Holy Spirit. His Father forgave those who crucified his Son. Jesus Christ suffered the agony of crucifixion, death, and hell for us. We, being crucified and buried with him by baptism into death, as Christ was raised from the dead by the glory of God, so were we. Unforgiveness was taken to hell in the body and soul of Jesus Christ and left there. He is the resurrection and the life. Living in Christ means forgiving and forgiving and forgiving and not allowing the oppressor to cause us to serve and obey sin. When asked by Peter, how often shall my brother sin against me, and I forgive him, Jesus answered, 'Until seventy times seven.'

Hebrews chapter 6, verses 4 through 8, tell us that it is impossible for those who have experienced the following, to turn their back on the goodness of God deliberately. Those that can turn away to renew themselves again to repentance, never really experienced it in the first place.

- They were once spiritually enlightened

- Given the understanding of saving knowledge

- Have experienced the heavenly gift

- Were made partakers of the Holy Ghost

- Have experienced the good Word of God

- The inherent power of the world to come, moral power, the excellence of soul, and the ability to perform miracles

By rejecting all that Christ has provided, they are treating his death, burial, and resurrection as though they were not saved by it and are again freshly crucifying the Son of God in their own souls, putting him to an open shame.

For the sake of your body and mind, you cannot afford to let emotions kindled and fired by unforgiveness drive you. The definition of unforgiveness is unwilling or unable to forgive. It is a matter of the heart. Medical books classify unforgiveness as a deadly disease. When you refuse to forgive, you unknowingly are taking radicle action against your body's health, your progress in life's situations, and you hinder others by your thoughts, words, and actions. Blatantly refusing to forgive makes you sick in a variety of ways. Until you decide to release from your heart the people or situations you are holding in unforgiveness, you will remain in adverse conditions.

The result of forgiveness is like the earth soaking up the rain that waters it repeatedly, producing crops useful for the benefit of those who cultivate it, receiving the goodness of God. With your cooperation, the blessings you receive daily, will solve problems, and heal your life. But unforgiveness in the same soil produces thorny plants and prickly wild plants that are hurtful to you and others. When you refuse to forgive, keep these possibilities in mind. Some consequences of unforgiveness are loss of your walk with God, damage of health and vitality, loss of joy, and loss of freedom by being consumed with, controlled by, and ultimately becoming like your offender. Other consequences are loss of hope, loss of future generations' health, and loss of your choice to trust God. Some warning signs of unforgiveness are bursts of anger, pettiness, impulsive, compulsive, uncontrolled negative feelings, sickness, recounting the offenses, hatred toward yourself or others, replaying the scene repeatedly, gossiping, feeling righteous and entitled, exercising poor judgment, and refusing help. The land has become of no value and close to being condemned. The only thing to do is burn it clean.

Remember, your spirit is one with the Spirit of God. Your soul is the turnstile from your spirit to your body. The make-up of your soul is your mind, will, emotions, intellect, and imagination. Your conscious and subconscious mind includes reason, memory, intuition, and perception. God invites you to reason with him by learning to think like him. To change your thinking and maintain the new thoughts, you must accept and develop a new perception that produces the desired results. Use your intuition to warn you of vacillating thoughts and your sense of awareness to capture and stop their effects on your emotions. To block God's power from flowing freely to sustain your life by harboring unforgiveness is to refuse access to your promises by refusing his divine nature. There are no other commandments greater than God's two commandments to love. Love the Lord your God with all your heart, all your soul, all your mind and all your strength. Secondly, love your neighbor as you love yourself. To love, in this manner, may sound challenging until you realize the consequences of protecting an unforgiving heart. Forgiveness is not active or accepted until you learn to forgive from your heart. The dynamic power, called excellence of soul power, released in your heart by the Holy Spirit to purify and heal, flows into every part of your body. You must guard, protect, and maintain your heart with all diligence because the source of life flows out of it.

How do you forgive from your heart? John the Baptist in Matthew chapter 3, verses 11 and 12, speaking of Jesus Christ said, 'He that comes after me is mightier than I, whose shoes I am not worthy to bear. He shall baptize you with the Holy Ghost, and with fire. His fan is in his hand, and he will thoroughly purge his floor, and gather his wheat into the garner, but he will burn up the chaff with unquenchable fire.' What does this mean concerning your heart? Jesus said, 'Every plant, which my heavenly Father has not planted, shall be rooted up.' As you learned previously, the production of spiritual fruit is crucial to obtaining the precious promises God has already given you. Picture your spirit which surrounds your soul and body as the atmosphere of your realm. The elements contained in your soul affect your heart and, therefore, your body. In your domain, your heart is the garden that provides food for your soul. It is your responsibility to work with the Holy Spirit and the ministering angels of God to cultivate and protect your heart.

The Holy Spirit draws your attention to and makes you aware of the warning signs and consequences of unforgiveness in your life. Always providing you with a choice, he shows you the results of cultivating the weeds of your heart and allows you to watch the reruns of negative thoughts, imaginations, and resultant emotions. They can only continue to produce the same feelings and driven actions that only serve to strengthen the consequences of unforgiveness. Once you decide to resist this pattern of negativity to take your freedom, the Holy Spirit leads you to remove the weeds from the soil of your heart systematically.

God is almighty, all-knowing, and his presence is everywhere. His love is alive in you and surrounds you right now. No power can overthrow his kingdom in you. The weeds he did not plant in your heart can be pulled up by the roots and burned by Jesus Christ, who is the Word of God. Hebrews chapter12, verse 29, says, 'For our God is a consuming fire.' Purify your soul with the Word of God by resisting the familiar reruns of the scene in your imagination that cause hurt and pain. As they come to you in the form of thoughts, stop them immediately. Thoughts do not have authority over you! Take control! Do not allow the scene to restart. Do not let them continue until they produce feelings that overwhelm you. If you have to, stop your imagination again and again until you are in control. Then quiet your mind by forcing yourself to think of something unrelated and pleasant. Speaking an amusing comment out loud will give you some light-hearted relief. You may have to repeat this process a few times until you gain control of your thoughts, even for a few seconds. Gaining control of your thoughts is your part and is only the beginning.

Every plant, which is a system or structure of an accumulation of opinions called a paradigm, in your heart that does not reflect God's divine nature must be rooted up and replaced by planting the proceeding Word of God. The proceeding Word of God is what the Holy Spirit is speaking to you or showing you now. Use what he shows you or speaks to you to replace the elements of the scene that are causing hurt and pain. The authority is in the name of Jesus, not how loud or how forceful your voice is. Jesus and his name are in you. By faith, believe the words you speak are alive, are sharper than any two-edged sword, and are happening now in the spiritual realm of your heart. Fill in the blanks according to what you've agreed should be pulled up and then say what the angels are planting in its place. Say the following, "In the name of Jesus, angels, pull up _____ (Ex. What someone said, how they embarrassed you, something you did or said, guilt, grief, physical pain, a lie, lack) by the roots, and plant _____ " (Ex. Love, peace, joy, I'm healed, the bill is paid, job). Out of a grateful heart, say, "Thank you, Father."

Receive God's love, peace, and joy by relaxing in the light of his presence. His presence is always here and now. Feel the warmth of God's love replenishing your heart. If you do not feel anything, know that faith does not work by feelings, but by love.

There is no reason to think or feel that nothing has changed. God is love. Be assured that the exchange has taken place in your heart. Do not let doubt and unbelief enter into your words or imagination, because you think you have to feel something. There is no power that is greater than God in you. When you love and believe God with 'all,' no matter what happens in your life, there is no reason to doubt.

The resisting has not ended because the 'thing' will come to test you. Remember, the pulling up of the old, and planting of the new is past tense in Jesus' name. You are in control of what you will allow or disallow into the garden of your heart. Do not accept the lie. Use your God-given imagination to imagine heavenly lifestyles and their associated feelings only. The stronger your genuine emotions of joy and gratitude become, because you have what you desire now, they will create an atmosphere of gladness and produce what you have planted. Working with the Holy Spirit and the angels to move through the process of forgiving is the beginning of pursuing a deeper relationship with him.

To live and move in the spiritual realm, learn to live by your spiritual senses. They are seeing, hearing, touching, tasting, smelling, and knowing or intuition. Forgiveness is vital in agreeing with, and living life, God's way. It increases your sensitivity to the Holy Spirit's leading. Learning to use your senses gives you awareness, perception, and foreknowledge of any situation or circumstance, enabling you to be fruitful, multiply, replenish, subdue, and having dominion over your garden and all the earth by releasing the power of God.

To hear the Holy Spirit's voice more clearly, daily experiencing the reality of his presence, pursue a deeper relationship with him. Deciding to love your enemies and consistently forgive, clears the way for the Holy Spirit to develop your senses and intuition. An entrance into the everlasting kingdom of your Lord and Savior Jesus Christ opens to you abundantly. Living in one accord with God defines your position, sets your destination, and builds his strategy to step your way into the course and purpose for your life. Develop your senses to quickly discern the will of God knowing that Jesus Christ is the way, the truth, and the life versus the manipulative systems of the world based on the knowledge of good and evil.

PART 3: THE PLAN

Chapter 7

Summary Questions

&

Reference Scriptures

PART 3: THE PLAN
Chapter 7 Summary Questions

Increase in Spiritual Strength and Power
Close Doors to Negative Thoughts, Words, and Actions

1. Why is learning from God, in the realm of heaven, two-sided?

2. Why is it crucial for you to close the doors to negative thoughts, words, and actions by forgiving?

3. Who is in control of whether you forgive or not?

4. What effect can unforgiveness, if persisted in, have on your body?

5. Why does God make a point of pulling up the plants he did not plant in you?

6. Has the Holy Spirit drawn your attention to one or more warning signs of unforgiveness in your life?

7. Decide to forgive one person or situation that continues to affect you negatively. By faith, what would you use your authority to say, and why?

8. Why is developing and living by your spiritual senses so important?

9. How important to you is spending time with the Holy Spirit?

10. Knowing that Jesus Christ is the way, the truth, and the life, are you able to discern the deception of the world's knowledge of good and evil?

Chapter 7 Scripture References
Descriptive Notes Taken from the Scripture for Research

Forgive from the Heart

Matthew 5:43-45
Love your enemies, bless them that curse you; that you may be the children of your Father which is in heaven.

Luke 23:33-35
Then said Jesus, Father, forgive them.

Matthew 18:22, 35
I say not unto you, until seven times: but, until seventy times seven. From your hearts, forgive.

Isaiah 53:10-12
Yet it pleased the LORD to bruise him; he hath put him to grief.

No More a Prey

Ezekiel 34:28-29
They shall no more be a prey to the heathen; neither shall the beast of the land devour them.

Preeminence

Colossians 1:12-20
He has the preeminence in all things. For it pleased the Father that in him should all fullness dwell.

Romans 6:3-6
We are buried with him by baptism into death that the body of sin might be destroyed. From here on, we should not serve sin.

Love the Lord with All

Isaiah 1:18-19
Come now, and let us reason together, says the LORD. If you be willing and obedient, you shall eat the good of the land.

Matthew 22:37-40
You shall love the Lord your God with all your heart, soul, and mind. Love your neighbor as yourself.

Purify Your Souls

Matthew 3:10-12
Whose fan is in his hand, and he will thoroughly purge his floor.

Matthew 15:12-14
Every plant, which my heavenly Father hath not planted, shall be rooted up.

I Peter 1:22
You have purified your souls in obeying the truth through the Spirit.

I John 3:2-3
Every man that hath this hope in him purifies himself, even as he is pure.

Proverbs 4:23
Keep your heart with all diligence; for out of it are the issues of life.

Authority in the Name of Jesus

I John 4:4
Greater is he that is in you, than he that is in the world.

Mark 16:14-18
These signs shall follow them that believe. In my name shall they…

John 15:16-17
Whatsoever you shall ask of the Father in my name; he may give it to you.

Matthew 21:18-23
And all things, whatsoever you shall ask in prayer, believing, you shall receive.

Believe the Words You Speak

II Corinthians 4:13
I believed, and therefore have I spoken; we also believe, and therefore speak.

Mark 5:35-36
Be not afraid, only believe.

John 4:50
Go your way; your son lives. And the man believed the word that Jesus had spoken unto him, and he went his way.

Ministering Angels

Psalm 103:19-22
Bless you the LORD, all his hosts; you ministers that do his pleasure and all his works in all places of his dominion: bless the LORD, O my soul.

Matthew 4:10-11
The devil left Jesus, and the angels came and ministered to him.

Mark 1:13
Jesus was there in the wilderness forty days, tempted of Satan; and was with the wild beasts; and the angels ministered to him.

Hebrews 1:14
Are they not all ministering spirits, sent forth to minister for them who shall be heirs of salvation?

Hebrews 12:22
But you have come to mount Sion, to the city of the living God, the heavenly Jerusalem, and an innumerable company of angels.

Resist the Enemy

James 4:7
Submit yourselves therefore to God. Resist the devil, and he will flee from you.

II Corinthians 10:3-6
Casting down imaginations, and bringing into captivity every thought to the obedience of Christ.

PART 4: STRATEGIC PREPARATION

Position

CHAPTER 8

Kingdom of God Governmental Authority

Increasing His Government and Peace Now and Forever

The boy's realization of total control, planned and managed by the puppet master who had planted malnourished weeds of manipulated knowledge in his heart, became evident the moment he heard God's voice. Spiritual blindness and failure, generated by his lack of opportunity to believe, created trauma in his heart. His oppressor systematically developed and effectively increased his trauma until its power had suppressed every part of his life. Forgiving himself and others from his heart, delivered the boy from 'living' with the effects of hopelessness caused by painful memories. Now, with Christ in God, he is free of the puppet master, his forceful oppression, and constant trauma. The atmosphere he once 'lived' in is gone.

Still standing in the love and light of God's presence, power, and glory, no longer controlled by his inability to decide or express himself, he looks around and takes several steps forward. Thinking about the numerous opportunities for change he observed on the earth, the boy's two questions remain. 'Where is my life going, and how do I get there from here?' Knowing his progress, God answers his thoughts, "Awareness, freedom, and transformation, have changed your life. By resting in me, you developed a deeper relationship with the Holy Spirit and learned how to produce his fruit from your spirit and soul. From your heart, you have learned how to forgive."

Continuing, God answers his question, "Where is your life going, and how will you get there from here? Now you will learn to position yourself strategically in the authority and power of my kingdom and its government. As you walk through life, fulfill my Word, 'As it is in heaven, so let it be on earth.' The Holy Spirit's knowledge is inexhaustible. Use your senses to follow him. Learn the ways of my Son's kingdom on earth. As you progressively act on what you have learned, the Holy Spirit will guide you onto your path. The glory of my presence will be with you in peace and power as you live the things you have both learned and received, and do what you have heard and seen. With each decision you make, the Holy Spirit will show you its completion, navigate your way, then, direct, correct, and guide you to your destination. To finish strong, you need a name. I will call you, Gem, G – E - M."

Before Jesus was born, God gave him the throne of David and his kingdom, to order and establish with judgment and justice. God prophesied through Isaiah, saying, 'The government shall be upon his shoulder.' He called his name, Wonderful, Counsellor, The mighty God, The everlasting Father, and The Prince of Peace. Understanding the meanings of his given name represented in Isaiah chapter 9, verse 6, is only the tip of the iceberg. You need revelation from the Holy Spirit to relate to the power in each name and its authority. Offered here are descriptions only.

- Wonderful means a miracle, a marvelous thing, and is God's acts of judgment and redemption.

- Counselor means to advise, consult, counsel, determine, devise, guide, purpose, and plan.

- Mighty in the name, The mighty God says powerful, warrior, champion, chief, excel, giant, mighty, strong, valiant, and brave.

- God means goodly, great, power, strong, god-like, mighty one, and strength.

- In the name, The everlasting Father, everlasting, is forever, continuing future and continuous existence.

- Father is originator, producer, generator, benevolence, and protection.

- In the name, Prince of Peace is the ruler, leader, captain, general, head, and overseer of Shalom.

- Peace is Shalom. Shalom means well, happy, friendly, welfare, health, prosperity, favor, perfect, rest, safety, wholly, completeness, soundness, quiet, tranquility, contentment, friendship (covenant), and peace from war.

As a child, Jesus grew strong in spirit, filled with wisdom, and the grace of God was on him. Developing a close relationship with his Father, Jesus learned Jewish teaching, culture, and practice in the Law of God, called the Torah. Progressively learning to live by what he heard and learned in the scriptures, he developed his spiritual senses to discern the things of God versus what he saw and heard from the actions of people around him. Through the Davidic Covenant, he would soon receive the throne and kingdom of David from his Father with the responsibility of continuing in them forever.

Through Solomon, David's son, God established David's house, kingdom, and throne forever. The Davidic Covenant received and prophesied to King David by Nathan the prophet, is eternal and unconditional based on God's faithfulness and mercy. God's covenant, accepted by King David promised:

- The Land and God's People – God will appoint a place and plant his people, so they have a home, live in peace, and move no more. (From the Abrahamic and Mosaic Covenants)

- David's House, Kingdom, and Throne – God will establish David a house, kingdom, and throne forever before him by allowing Solomon to succeed him as king of Israel.

- Kingdom – God will establish Solomon's kingdom.

- Throne – God will establish Solomon's throne forever through Jesus Christ.

- Government – Israel will be a people governed by a king's rule and authority that they might be unto me for a people, and a name, and for a praise, and a glory.

- Son – God will be Solomon's father, and Solomon shall be his son.

- God's House – Solomon built a house for God's name. When the instruments and singers praised as one, God filled the temple with his glory cloud.

- Mercy – God's mercy will not depart away from Solomon. God will settle Solomon in his house and his kingdom forever.

To carry out God's purpose, Jesus Christ ordered and established his kingdom and government with judgment and justice on the throne and kingdom of David, to align with his Father's kingdom rule and throne in heaven. He set his government and peace by the prophecy that proceeded him, to increase from that time on and forever. The scripture says, 'The zeal of the LORD of hosts will perform this.'

What does it mean for you that his government, which means realm, dominion, and sovereignty, is ordered and established with judgment and justice? An ordered and established government is one of strength that, when appropriately set up in a variety of applications, is prepared to meet, support, harmoniously arrange, sustain, and provide while upholding the sovereignty of the throne. Judgment and justice are the foundation of God's throne. Mercy, loving-kindness, and truth appear wherever he is. Together, judgment and justice, are righteousness saying, 'as it should be.' As it should be, is changing all the changeable things the boy could see on the earth through the two-way open-ended lens to align with the goodness of the kingdom of God.

God prepares John the Baptist for the end of his ministry. Not knowing who his successor would be, John sees himself baptizing the man in the water and the Spirit descending from heaven like a dove and resting on him. God told John that the one whom he would see the Spirit descending on, and remaining, is the same one who baptizes with the Holy Ghost. John baptized with water. Jesus baptizes with the Holy Spirit and fire. For the two of them to fulfill all righteousness, John baptizes Jesus in the Jordan River. As he comes straight up out of the water praying, the heavens open, and he sees the Spirit of God descending like a dove and remaining on him. His Father voices his approval by speaking from heaven, "This is my beloved Son, in whom I am well pleased. Hear him."

Immediately being full of the Holy Spirit, Jesus is led into the wilderness by the Holy Spirit. The God-appointed leader of his kingdom government and the self-appointed leader of the kingdom government of darkness face-off in the wilderness. Fasting for 40 days, being tempted by the devil, Jesus has eaten nothing. Satan uses his arsenal of three temptations in various forms to try to deceive and control Jesus. For Jesus to give in to the devil's will and way at any point concedes defeat. Spiritually adept at using his awareness, senses, and the authority of the spoken Word of

God, Jesus is more than a match for Satan. Satan challenges his Sonship, his position with his Father. Then he tries to kill him by misusing the intent of God's Word against him. Using the 'you shall not surely die' deception, he tries to convince Jesus to initiate a life or death situation with his angels. By putting his life at risk to challenge the Word of God, he removes himself from the protection of dwelling in his Father. If Jesus gives in to the intimidation, he is not only challenging his Father, but he is displacing himself since he is the Word of God. Taking the lust of the pride of life to the lowest level, he would place himself in the hands of Satan and under the authority of his voice.

Tempting Jesus with the lust of the flesh, the devil, knowing that his body is weak from fasting, tries to use his position as the Son of God against him. He challenges him by saying, 'if you are the Son of God,' and then tells him to command that the stones around him turn into bread. In other words, obey my voice to prove your position and authority to me. Jesus says, 'It is written, man shall not live by bread alone, but by every word that proceeds out of the mouth of God.'

For the devil's second temptation, he questions Jesus' position with his Father. He takes Jesus up into a high mountain and shows him all the kingdoms of the world in a moment of time. These kingdoms legally belong to him because Adam gave him control of them to do with as he wishes. He uses the lust of the eyes to offer him all their power and glory. Satan's condition involves worship. He tells Jesus directly that the only way he can get the kingdoms of the world and their glory is to 'fall at his feet and worship him.' Jesus responds by telling Satan to get behind him. Then he says, 'It is written, you shall worship the Lord your God, and him only shall you serve.'

Satan then uses the pride of life for the third temptation. He tries to convince Jesus to trust himself with his life rather than his Father. Taking him to Jerusalem, the holy city, he sets him on a pinnacle of the temple. His question to him is, 'If thou be the Son of God, jump down from here. It is written, He shall give his angels charge over you, to keep you and in their hands, they shall bear you up, lest at any time you dash your foot against a stone.' Jesus answered him, saying, 'It is said, you shall not tempt the Lord your God.' After this response from Jesus, the devil ended his temptations and left. The angels came and ministered to him. For Jesus, spiritual victory over the devil's three temptations translated to the following. My Father and I are One. My position and authority agree with his, not yours. I love and worship my Father by obeying his voice only. Satan, we have come with an everlasting kingdom, throne, and government prepared to take all the kingdoms of the world and the glory of them from you and rule over.

When Jesus heard that John was in prison, he left Nazareth and traveled to Galilee, preaching the gospel of the kingdom of God. Jesus, the light of the world, began his three-year ministry in power. Expressing the judgment and justice of heaven, he preached the gospel of the kingdom saying, 'Repent for the kingdom of heaven is at hand.' At hand, announced the established presence of God's kingdom, throne, and operating government that is available now, in power and glory.

From the days of John the Baptist until the moment Jesus Christ began his ministry, the kingdom of heaven had suffered violence. Violence became possible on earth when Adam decided to follow the voice of Satan, instead of the voice of God. Jesus makes his intention clear when he says, 'Until now.' 'Now' is still in effect for you. He continues by saying that the violent take it by force. Jesus, knowing there is no time or distance in the spirit realm, demonstrates the increase of his government and peace by forcefully removing the influence of the enemy, healing the damage and restoring the kingdom.

What authority gave Jesus Christ the right to stop the uncontrolled suffering from violence in his presence by demanding peace? For Israel, he is the promised Messiah, who comes from the lineage of King David and the tribe of Judah, establishing an everlasting kingdom. Walking in the authority of the unconditional Davidic Covenant, Jesus announced his fulfillment of the prophecies that proceeded his birth and ministry. His alignment with his Father's throne in heaven, King David's throne on earth, and his baptism in the Holy Spirit enable him to release their authority in power to do the work of his kingdom.

Jesus maintained a close relationship with his Father through prayer and meditation. His spiritual ability to hear, say, and do according to the proceeding Word of his Father was evident. He lived by his senses, releasing the Holy Spirit's power to carry out his Father's will in both the heavenly realm and the earthly realm. Fasting keeps your spirit, soul, and body close to and open to receiving from the Spirit of God.

By faith, at any moment, in any situation, the power of God is available to restore peace. For people who are spiritually blinded by the enemy, adverse conditions consistently follow closed eyes and ears. Change cannot take place, even though God's presence, knowledge, and power are presently available for release. No faith results in no power released and no peace restored, unless God, in the sovereignty of his grace and mercy, acts on their behalf, as he did for the boy who 'lived,' being treated like a puppet.

Surrounded by the atmosphere of God's glory, Jesus taught, preached, healed, worked miracles, and delivered the oppressed. Why does the glory of the kingdom permeate his atmosphere even now? Jesus, immersed in the Holy Spirit, walks freely in the Law of Love. One hundred percent one with God in spirit, soul, and body, he visibly emanates the beauty of his presence. To the people who sit in darkness and the shadow of death, Jesus Christ represents the house of God filled with the cloud of his glory. The people that followed him experienced and received goodness and mercy from the kingdom government residing in him.

When Jesus fulfilled his ministry, he was sacrificed willingly on the cross of Calvary, receiving, and suffering for the sin of humanity. Showing mercy, God made him sin for us. By the death, burial, and resurrection of Jesus Christ, God reconciled all things to himself through his everlasting covenant, ratified by the pure Blood of Jesus. The New Covenant extends God's mercy, righteousness, and the abundance of grace. By the forgiveness of sins and redemption of all humanity, God restored the heaven and earth connection through his Son Jesus Christ, the kingdoms, and the fullness of the earth. For you in the body of Christ, his covenant also restores his kingdom, throne, and government within you. Reborn by the Holy Spirit, you are now his child learning sonship from the Holy Spirit in his household. With salvation comes the ministry of the Holy Spirit, the direct activity of God's archangels and their hosts of angels, and the guaranteed promises of God.

After his resurrection, Jesus taught his disciples for forty days, showing himself alive to them by many infallible proofs and speaking with them concerning the things of the kingdom of God. He demonstrated the power and way of the kingdom, telling them to wait for the Father's promise, the Holy Spirit, whom he would send after his ascension. John the Baptist baptized them with water, but now baptized with the Holy Ghost and fire, they would receive the power prophesied in the book of Joel chapter 2, verse 28. God will pour out his Spirit upon all flesh. Their sons and daughters will prophesy, old men will dream dreams, and their young men will see visions. One hundred and twenty men and women continued in prayer, seeking God with one accord in the upper room until the day of Pentecost. Suddenly a sound from heaven came like a mighty rushing wind and filled the house where they were sitting. Cloven tongues like fire appeared to them, and sat upon each one, filled them with the Holy Ghost, and they began to speak with other tongues as the Spirit spoke through them.

The Lord Jesus Christ received all power in heaven and in the earth. God set Jesus at his own right hand in heavenly places, far above all principality, power, might, dominion, and every name that is named, not only in this world but in the one to come. He put all things under his feet and made him the head over all things to the church, which is now his body, the fullness of him who makes everything complete, and who fills everything everywhere with himself.

The kingdom government of God, the supreme ruling authority, is now operating in the earth from God's throne in heaven. The New Covenant, established by Jesus Christ, who through the eternal Spirit, offered himself to God without spot provides forgiveness of sin, eternal life, restored fellowship with God your Father, and fruitful blessings. The Lord Jesus Christ, your Apostle, High Priest, and Intercessor fulfilled the law of the Old Covenant and is the Mediator of the New Covenant. Entering into the New Covenant is by faith in Jesus Christ. Upon doing so, God gives you a new heart to love and please him. His Spirit, the Spirit of Truth, lives with you and in you. Your body is now the temple of the Holy Spirit, and you are not your own. Glorify God in your body and spirit, which are bought with the Blood of Jesus and belong to God.

You are now on the resurrection side of the cross in the body of the Lord Jesus Christ. To you, God has made him, wisdom, righteousness, sanctification, and redemption. He witnessed the problems of the world from God's heart perspective. He said, 'If you can believe, with God, all things are possible.' Jesus Christ, the prince of the kings of the earth, made the disciples and you a king and a priest to God. You are now reborn into a chosen generation, a royal priesthood, a holy nation, and a purchased people by the Blood of Christ. With a grateful heart, show forth the praises of God who has called you out of darkness into his marvelous light. Believe in the name of Jesus and the power of his Blood. In him, you have the authority to use his name to overcome any adversity. You have the same glorious opportunity to represent his kingdom and government, because, like Jesus and his disciples, by the Holy Spirit, the kingdom of God with the authority of his ruling government is in you.

PART 4: STRATEGIC PREPARATION

Chapter 8

Summary Questions
&
Reference Scriptures

PART 4: STRATEGIC PREPARATION
Chapter 8 Summary Questions

Kingdom of God Governmental Authority
Increasing His Government and Peace Now and Forever

1. Why is the name given to Jesus in Isaiah chapter 9, verse 6, only the tip of the iceberg?

2. How did God establish King David's house, throne, and kingdom forever?

3. What made the Davidic Covenant unconditional?

4. How did God prepare John the Baptist for the end of his ministry?

5. What are some variations of three temptations the devil uses? Give examples, and what Word you would use to overcome the temptations?

6. Using the authority of the force of faith in that same Word, do you know how to take back that part of your life?

7. Why is the presence and power of God always available?

8. What is the way of the kingdom of God?

9. Jesus said, 'If you can believe, all things are possible.' List some things you once thought were unchangeable, that you now plan to change.

10. Has your understanding of what it means to be in the body of the Lord Jesus Christ changed?

Chapter 8 Scripture References
Descriptive Notes Taken from the Scripture for Research

When I Make Up My Jewels

Malachi 3:16-18
And they shall be mine, says the LORD of hosts, in that day when I make up my jewels.

I Peter 2:1-6
Ye also, as lively stones, are built up a spiritual house, a holy priesthood, to offer up spiritual sacrifices, acceptable to God by Jesus Christ.

As it is In Heaven

Matthew 6:10
Your kingdom come, your will be done in earth, as it is in heaven.

The Government is On His Shoulder

Isaiah 7:14
Therefore the Lord himself shall give you a sign; Behold, a virgin shall conceive, and bear a son, and shall call his name Immanuel.

Isaiah 9:6-7
Unto us a son is given: and the government shall be upon his shoulder. The zeal of the LORD of hosts will perform this.

Isaiah 11:1-5
A rod comes out of the stem of Jesse. A Branch shall grow out of his roots.

Matthew 21:9
Hosanna to the son of David: Blessed is he that comes in the name of the Lord.

Revelation 3:7
He has the key of David. He opens, and no man shuts; and shuts, and no man opens.

The Child Grew

Luke 1:40
The child grew, and waxed strong in spirit, filled with wisdom.

The Davidic Covenant – God's Kingdom Government Aligned

The Land and God's People – Heaven, Earth and God's People

II Samuel 7:10
I will appoint a place for my people Israel. That they may dwell in a place of their own.

Jeremiah 13:11
I caused to cleave to me the whole house of Israel and the whole house of Judah, says the LORD; that they might be unto me for a people, a name, a praise, and a glory.

Jeremiah 31:31, 33
I will make a new covenant with the house of Israel, and the house of Judah. I will put my law in their inward parts, and write it in their hearts.

Ezekiel 36:26-30
A new heart also will I give you, and a new spirit will I put within you. You shall dwell in the land I gave your fathers. You shall be my people, and I will be your God.

Psalm 115:15-16
The heavens, are the LORD's: but the earth he has given to the children of men.

Romans 4:13-14
For the promise, that he should be the heir of the world, was to Abraham, through faith.

Hebrews 1:2
Has spoken unto us by his Son, whom he has appointed heir of all things.

Acts 10:42-48
Through his name whosoever believeth in him shall receive remission of sins. While Peter yet spoke these words, the Holy Ghost fell on all them which heard the word.

Ephesians 2:13-15
But now in Christ Jesus you who sometimes were far off are made nigh by the blood of Christ. For he is our peace, who hath made both one in himself.

Hebrews 9:14-15, 23-28
He is the mediator of the new testament. Now once in the end of the world has he appeared to put away sin by the sacrifice of himself.

I Corinthians 6:14-20
Your body is the temple of the Holy Ghost which is in you, which you have of God, and you are not your own? Glorify God in your body, and in your spirit, which are God's.

I Peter 2:9
You are a chosen generation, a royal priesthood, a holy nation, a peculiar people; that you should shew forth the praises of him who hath called you into his marvelous light.

David's House, Kingdom, Throne
God's House, Kingdom, Throne

II Samuel 7:11, 16
Also the LORD tells you that he will make you a house established forever before you.

II Chronicles 5:1-14
Solomon finished the house of the LORD. The glory cloud of the LORD filled the house.

Ephesians 2:18-22
Now you are fellow citizens with the saints, and of the household of God.

Romans 14:17
The kingdom of God is righteousness, peace and joy in the Holy Ghost.

Luke 17:21-22
Behold, the kingdom of God is within you.

I Chronicles 29:11-13
All that is in the heaven and in the earth is yours. LORD you are exalted head above all.

Psalm 89:14
Justice and judgment are the habitation of your throne: mercy and truth go before you.

Psalm 103:19
The LORD has prepared his throne in the heavens; and his kingdom rules over all.

Psalm 45:6
The scepter of your kingdom is a right scepter.

God Established Solomon's Throne

I Chronicles 17:11-12
David, I will raise up your son and establish the throne of his kingdom forever.

Hebrews 1:8
To the Son, Your throne is forever. Your kingdom is a scepter of righteousness.

David's Son Solomon – God's Son Jesus Christ

I Chronicles 17:13-14
I will be his father, and he shall be my son.

Hebrews 1:1-6
You are my Son. And again, I will be to him a Father, and he shall be to me a Son?

God's Mercy toward David – God's Mercy toward Humanity

II Samuel 7:15
But my mercy shall not depart away from him, as I took it from Saul.

Acts 13:34-37
I will give you the sure mercies of David. God shall not suffer his Holy One to see corruption.

Romans 8:34
It is Christ that died, yea rather, that is risen again, who is even at the right hand of God, who also makes intercession for us.

Hebrews 2:14-15
He became flesh and blood that through death he might destroy the devil that had the power of death, and deliver them who through fear of death were subject to bondage.

Hebrews 2:16-18
He was made like his brethren, that he might be a merciful and faithful high priest in things pertaining to God, to make reconciliation for the sins of the people.

Hebrews 3:1
Wherefore, holy brethren, partakers of the heavenly calling, consider the Apostle and High Priest of our profession, Christ Jesus.

We Are Kings and Priests

Revelation 1:5-6
Jesus Christ, the prince of the kings of the earth, has made us kings and priests unto God and his Father.

Revelation 5:9-10
And has made us unto our God kings and priests: and we shall reign on the earth.

John and Jesus Fulfill All Righteous

Matthew 3:13-17
Then comes Jesus from Galilee to Jordan to John, to be baptized of him. Suffer it to be so now: for thus it becomes us to fulfil all righteousness.

3 Temptations Government Face-Off in the Wilderness

Luke 4:1-2
Jesus being full of the Holy Ghost returned from Jordan, and was led by the Spirit into the wilderness.

Hebrews 5:14
But strong meat belongs to those who by reason of use have their senses exercised to discern both good and evil.

I John 2:16
For all that is in the world, the lust of the flesh, and the lust of the eyes, and the pride of life, is not of the Father, but is of the world.

The Lust of the Flesh

Luke 4:3-4
The devil said, 'If you are the Son of God, command this stone that it be made bread.'

The Lust of the Eyes

Luke 4:5-8
The devil said, 'All this power and glory will I give you, if you will worship me.'

The Pride of Life

Luke 4:9-12
He brought him to Jerusalem, and set him on a pinnacle of the temple. The devil said, 'If you are the Son of God, cast yourself down.'

Devil Ended All 3 of his Temptation

Luke 4:13
And when the devil had ended all the temptation, he departed from him for a season.

The Kingdom of Heaven is at Hand

John 8:12
I am the light of the world. He that follows me shall not walk in darkness, but shall have the light if life.

Matthew 4:16-17
The people which sat in darkness and in the shadow of death saw great light. From that time Jesus began to preach, and to say, 'Repent: for the kingdom of heaven is at hand.'

Mark 1:14-15
After John was put in prison, Jesus came into Galilee, saying, the time is fulfilled, and the kingdom of God is at hand: repent ye, and believe the gospel.

Take the Kingdom by Force

Matthew 11:12
And from the days of John the Baptist until now the kingdom of heaven suffers violence, and the violent take it by force.

Luke 16:16
The law and the prophets were until John: since that time the kingdom of God is preached, and every man presses into it.

What Authority did Jesus Christ Possess?

Jeremiah 23:5
Behold, the days come, says the LORD, that I will raise unto David a righteous Branch, and a King shall reign and prosper, and shall execute judgment and justice in the earth.

Isaiah 11:1-2
And there shall come forth a rod out of the stem of Jesse, and a Branch shall grow out of his roots. And the spirit of the LORD shall rest upon him.

Luke 1:31-32
You shall call his name Jesus. He shall be great, and shall be called the Son of the Highest: and the Lord God shall give unto him the throne of his father David.

Luke 1:33, 69
He shall reign over the house of Jacob forever; and of his kingdom there shall be no end. God has raised up a horn of salvation for us in the house of his servant David.

The Anointed Jesus

Luke 4:18-19
The Spirit of the Lord is upon me, because he hath anointed me.

Luke 4:16-21
He closed the book, and sat down, saying, 'This day is this scripture fulfilled in your ears.'

John 3:12-13
No man hath ascended up to heaven, but he that came down from heaven, even the Son of man which is in heaven.

The Marveled at Their Unbelief

Mark 6:4-6
He could only heal a few sick folk. He marveled because of their unbelief.

The New Blood Covenant

Hebrews 13:20-21
God of peace brought again from the dead our Lord Jesus, through the blood of the everlasting covenant.

Colossians 1:14
In whom we have redemption through his blood, even the forgiveness of sins.

Hebrews 10:9-10
I come to do your will, O God. He taketh away the first that he may establish the second.

Not Held Accountable for Past Sin

John 3:15-18
God sent not his Son into the world to condemn the world; but that the world through him might be saved.

Romans 8:1-2
There is therefore now no condemnation to them which are in Christ Jesus. The law of the Spirit of life in Christ Jesus hath made me free from the law of sin and death.

II Corinthians 5:18-19
And all things are of God, who hath reconciled the world to himself by Jesus Christ, not imputing their trespasses unto them

II Corinthians 5:21
For he made him to be sin for us, who knew no sin; that we might be made the righteousness of God in him.

I Corinthians 1:30
Christ Jesus is made unto us wisdom, and righteousness, and sanctification, and redemption.

Restoration of the Heaven and Earth Connection

Hebrews 12:22-24
You are come to the city of the living God, the heavenly Jerusalem and to Jesus the mediator of the new covenant.

Jesus Showed Himself Alive by Many Infallible Proofs

Acts 1:2-5, 8
He shewed himself alive by many infallible proofs. You shall receive power.

Acts 2:1-4
On the day of Pentecost the Holy Ghost came, filled them and they spoke in tongues.

Acts 2:16-18
It shall come to pass in the last days, says God, I will pour out of my Spirit upon all flesh.

John 21:25
Many other things which Jesus did, the world itself could not contain the books.

All Power in the Name of Jesus

Matthew 28:18-20
Jesus said, 'All power is given unto me in heaven and in earth.'

Ephesians 1:20-23
God set Jesus far above all principality, power, might, dominion, and every name.

Colossians 1:16-17
For by him were all things created, that are in heaven, and that are in earth.

Believe, All Things Are Possible

Mark 9:23
If thou canst believe, all things are possible to him that believes.

CHAPTER 9

Holy Spirit and the Weapons of Spiritual Warfare

Understanding Their Function and Use

After the resurrection, the Father sent the Holy Spirit to the earth in Jesus' name. Continuing the ministry of Jesus Christ, the Holy Spirit's assignment is to draw and convict people who are under the influence of the world system of sin because they do not believe in Jesus Christ, the Light of the world. He convicts the world of righteousness because Jesus Christ has finished his work and gone to his Father. Because the prince of this world is judged, the Holy Spirit draws unbelievers to the love of God and the light of eternal life provided by Jesus Christ, rather than remain in the darkness of timeless death with Satan and his angels. Seated together in heavenly places at the right hand of the Father with the now glorified Lord Jesus Christ, Gem now has the ministry of reconciliation.

Progressively using what he has heard, seen, and learned, Gem is learning to walk the course of his life with purpose in the spiritual and natural realms. To reach his destination, he prayerfully listens to the Holy Spirit as he studies the Word of God. Listening to his revelations and interpretations of the truth, Gem gains wisdom, knowledge, and understanding of his purpose. The Holy Spirit directs his path by showing him and preparing him for what lies ahead.

He informs Gem by saying, "Your position in heavenly places in Christ Jesus gives you the authority to use his name and the power of his Blood to overcome the enemy in every area of life. Worship your Father to receive revelation, knowledge, wisdom, and understanding in the elements of spiritual warfare before moving in the authority and power of eternal life, unconditional love, and pure light. Walk in the Life, Love, and Light of my glory. To fulfill your purpose, you must learn who you are in him and what your spiritual weapons are. Know them, and how to release them in power to do your Father's will." After a moment, the Holy Spirit speaks to him again, "Gem." Gem responds, "Yes, Holy Spirit?" The Holy Spirit encourages him, "Shine as a light in the world!"

Your ultimate example of a spiritual weapon is the Lord Jesus Christ at the right hand of the throne of God. He is One with his Father, who is eternal life, unconditional love, and pure light. Translated into his kingdom by the Holy Spirit, you inherited all that Jesus Christ restored by overcoming the world and its prince, the devil. In Jesus Christ, you become a spiritual weapon. Learn what your spiritual weapons are, and use them to fill your life, your atmosphere, environment, surroundings, and the earth with the goodness God originally intended for humanity. How? Follow the example of creation in the beginning, when God the Father, his Son, the spoken Word, and the movement of the Holy Spirit created the heavens and the earth. God made decisions concerning his design, and then saw all the elements interacting together before the Holy Spirit moved over the surface of the waters. Just as God's presence moved on the deep waters, forming what God saw, his presence moves on you when his will forms in you. Then God spoke the Word saying, "Let there be light." He actually commanded the out of the darkness by saying, "Light be!" The scripture says, 'And there was light.' In John chapter 10, verse 34, Jesus answered them, "Is it not written in your law, I said, You are gods?" Become imitators of God. Walk as children of light, commanding and releasing his light.

When you believe the spiritual realm is real, and with repetition, you can accomplish up to 99% of the decision you make in your spirit and soul, then on-going manifestations are imminent. Make this way of living a lifestyle. Develop the ability to step into the result of what you desire visually and live from there. Align your thoughts, emotions, feelings, conversation, and actions, fully living your desire in your imagination 24/7 until the outcome becomes your new normal. Using your imagination, become diligent at creating your desire while at the same time, guarding it against old thoughts and feelings. If you allow the thoughts that are associated with your former way of life to enter into your mind by thinking them, you give them strength and impose an unchangeable stand-off. Thinking these thoughts create causes and effects to keep the old things you have decided to change in their place. Refuse to entertain those former thoughts, feel the old emotions, or speak, and act in a manner that you no longer desire. Give strength and increased power to what you imagine within by agreeing with it as you live your daily life. Be strong and courageous in Christ. Live and walk in the Spirit. Use your God-given imagination to align your lifestyle with the will of God.

Jesus Christ, the ultimate weapon of light, focused his thinking and power on the result he desired, rather than on what faced him at the moment. How did he know beforehand what the result would be? He spent time in prayer and meditation with his Father and received his will for each situation. How did he know what to say or do? Jesus remained in constant communication with the Holy Spirit, who knows everything past, present, and future. Listening to the Holy Spirit, he spoke and acted toward the result he desired. It was and still is his choice to speak the Word, expecting the situation to align with his Word just as it is yours. You are the temple of the Holy Spirit. He is here on the earth, along with God's angels, to assist you. His power is available to help you face and overcome any opposition. Knowing this is especially important because you are here to fulfill the written volume of your book in heaven. Just as Jesus fulfilled God's plan for his life, you are here to carry out God's victorious plan for your life in victory.

To accomplish God's plan for your life, you need his weapons of light to dispel and overcome the planned attacks of the kingdom of darkness and its defeated ruler. Because you are one with the Father, Jesus Christ, and the Holy Spirit, knowing what weapons of warfare you have within you is just the beginning. See yourself in the glorified Christ as he is now, the head of the church, with all power. He has overcome the world. Use the authority of Jesus' name and the cleansing power of his Blood to remain free of offense and unforgiveness, while continuing to manifest the fruit of the Spirit. Fasting strengthens your spirit, enabling you to hear the voice of the Holy Spirit more clearly and helps you keep your soul and body aligned with the will of God. With this understanding, walking in the increased flow of God's glorious power released by his offensive and defensive weapons enables you to stand against and quench the fiery attacks of the enemy. He tries to attack your thoughts with suggestions using his three temptations. As discussed, they are the lust of the flesh, the lust of the eyes, and the pride of life.

Ephesians chapter 6, verse 10, says, 'Finally, my brethren, be strong in the Lord and in the power of his might.' Remember, in the glorified Lord Jesus Christ, you are in the freedom of his life, love, and light. God created you in his image. Unveiling your heart in the mirror of glory of the Lord allows the Spirit to change you from one level of glory to the next into the same image of Christ. Being changed into the glorious image of the

Lord is a powerful thing. What will you do with his eternal life, unconditional love, and pure light in you? Develop them in you, increase in them, and then release their power in Jesus' name to enforce and or restore God's dominion over all the earth. Subdue the enemy's controlling and debilitating systems in his areas of influence along with the evil effects they produce. Then use your God-given dominion to be fruitful, multiply, and replenish these areas of death and manipulated destruction with the all-powerful glory of God's life, love, and light.

To allow the strength and power of the Holy Spirit to flow through you when needed, remove your attention from your ability. Focus on his power and then imagine the light of the glory flowing through you. To use his spiritual weapons effectively, relax, and receive from the Holy Spirit's wisdom, understanding, counsel, might, knowledge, and fear of the Lord, allowing the information to flow into your spirit. Continue to listen without self-talk, reasoning, or wondering with your thoughts and solutions. If necessary, ask questions for further clarification. The Holy Spirit will tell you or show you what you need to know. Letting peace reign in your heart is a vital part of learning how to use your spiritual weapons of warfare. There is no need to become anxious or agitated when you know the one who caused the problem is already defeated. The spiritual weapon you need for each situation is already in you. There are no surprises in the spirit realm. The Godhead is well aware of the enemy's tactics before he initiates them. Ask for wisdom, and receive the answer in peace.

Your defeated foe, the devil, acts, speaks, and takes it for granted that he can control your life at any moment. He approaches you in various ways, trying to insert his thoughts and then use them to control you at your points of mental and emotional weakness. For this reason, put on the whole armor of God, so you will be able to stand against the wiles of the devil. Take note, without God's armor; you will not be able to stand against principalities, powers, the rulers of the darkness of this world, and spiritual wickedness in high places. Why, because

Jesus Christ, the armor of light, has already defeated them. You can only stand against them in him. God has set him down at his right hand in heavenly places, far above all principality, power, might, dominion, and every name that is named, not only in this world but also in that which is to come. God put all things under Jesus' feet and made him the head over all things to the church, his body.

Ephesians chapter 6, verses 13, tells you to take unto you the whole armor of God that you may be able to withstand in the evil day. When thoughts come to move you out of his presence, seek the kingdom of God first and his righteousness. Then you will know what is essential for you to accomplish today without the pressure of a to-do list for tomorrow. There is sufficient evil to overcome daily. In God's presence, keep your thoughts on the moment at hand. Each piece of armor is representative of the Godhead. Redeemed by Jesus Christ, wearing the armor gives you the authority in his name, to move in dominion and resurrection power.

The remainder of verse 13 says, and having done all, to stand. What does this mean? The armor of light is two-sided. The continuous flow of the power of God flows through Jesus, the anointed One, and you by the Holy Spirit. The Holy Spirit has anointed you. Protect the power of your anointing from those who seek to weaken you. The light of the body is the eye. This flow of light requires a single eye view from all involved. To submit to God, who is light and no darkness at all, is to give yourself to him entirely; spirit, soul, and body. You have heard the phrase, 'there's no two ways about it.' Either God is your Father, or the devil is your father. You cannot be your own father. Jesus Christ redeemed you to live unto God, not to hold back something for yourself to control. Use the two-sided armor with the single eye of light from God. Above all, the Shield of Faith because it protects your life and purpose from the attacks of the old man's dead thinking that links you with the enemy's views. He tries to use his thoughts to deceive and force compromise. If you have not spiritually prepared your spirit, soul, and body by studying and applying the Word of God to your life with the Holy Spirit, there is no use putting the armor of light on, and trying to function in it. You will not know how to follow and flow with the Holy Spirit to release the light of God's glory and fight the good fight of faith to victory without it.

The Breastplate of Righteousness protects all things including grace, peace (Shalom), faith, love, and the abundance of joy in your heart. Understanding righteousness, which is right standing with God, restored by Jesus Christ for you, is key to using the name of Jesus and the power of his Blood to experience the goodness of God, halt the enemy, and obtain victory no matter what you face. Receive the gift of righteousness and the abundance of grace to reign in life by Jesus Christ. The expressed power of faith and love manifests the living Word in your heart and what you believe in your life. Sow the fruits of righteousness in peace. Make peace with pure wisdom from above, which is gentle, reasonable, and full of compassion and love.

The Helmet of Salvation protects your joint-heir inheritance in Christ concerning how you think, hear, see, smell, and speak. God gave you the spirit of power, love, and a sound mind. How you think, what you see, and say establishes changes in your atmosphere, surroundings, and environment. No longer are you alone in this world trying to figure out what to do next, and how to accomplish it against seemingly insurmountable competition and opposition.

The Holy Spirit communicates with you in various ways, including dreams and visions, which enable you to move forward spiritually, then personally in life. Be aware of your thoughts, words, actions, and surroundings during dreams and visions. While paying attention to what you see and hear, also take note of how the dreams and visions make you feel. Feeling uneasy or fearful is a warning sign. A realistic or specific dream may be pleasant, or one that makes you experience adversity. Take note of how what is taking place affects you. You can interact with the dream by changing how you think, respond, and do during the dream. Remaining aware of what is happening around you, helps you gather the information that may be helpful to you. It may provide you with details of upcoming events, or alert you to the activities of certain people in various situations.

Do not try to access or interpret the dream or vision by your-self. The Holy Spirit knows what is ahead for you, what you need to address or change in your life, or how to help others. Although dreams can seem very real while you are asleep, and some are, you can quickly forget them after you awake. Keep a notebook by your bed to write down the events of the dream that you feel are essential. As soon as possible, ask the Holy Spirit about the dream, then immediately write what he says and date it.

There are three types of visons; inner vision, open vision, and trance. You see an inner vision while you are awake. An inner vision can be a picture, image, or similar to a film clip. At first, you may think it's just a thought, but then you realize you are seeing an image or a flash of an event that is happening in your spirit. While looking at an open vision in front of you, you are still able to see and relate to your surroundings. During a trance, your natural senses are suspended, and you are only conscious of the spiritual realm. Awareness is vitally important. Relax and pay attention during the trance. If possible, ask the Holy Spirit questions about what you are seeing. Write down and date what you've seen, and what he says.

God, Jesus, and you can smell the words you speak. Immediately, you sense the purity of your thoughts and words, tasting them as they fill your belly. You live by what you see and imagine, speak into, and do in your environment. Think good thoughts. Speak all is well. Spend quiet time with the Holy Spirit to meditate and receive the events of your day, your next step in life, or what he desires for you to face and overcome. During meditation, listen to hear, and look to see. Forward-thinking is using your imagination to see the reality of the desired change while living in the presence of God. Receive, say, and do in the name of Jesus. Knowing and agreeing with what you have inher-ited protects you from the enemy's attacks. He cannot succeed against the power of your Word unless you give him your permission from a basis of wrong thinking.

Take the Sword of the Spirit, which is the word of God. Know the Word that pertains to the situation or circumstance that needs to be changed and then speak it from faith in your heart. If you don't know what scripture to use, ask the Holy Spirit for the one that applies. Believe the Word in your heart before you speak it over the problem in Jesus' name. If you don't believe what you say, nothing will happen. You found the scripture reference, and you can read the words, but there is no power coming from belief in your heart. The living Word is powerful and sharper than any two-edged sword. When spoken in faith, it cuts deep. It divides in two the soul and the spirit, the joints and the marrow, and it discerns the thoughts and intents of the heart. To experience the goodness of the Word, first, imagine it in your spirit. Then step the scripture through each part of your soul. See it come alive in your heart and then in your life. By doing this first, you are speaking the truth from a testimony lived in your heart, and not just because you heard someone else read the scripture.

Revelation chapter 1, verse 16, tells us, out of Jesus' mouth went a two-edged sword. You receive personal tongues from the Holy Spirit. Begin by expressing what you hear or see in your spirit, then yield to the Holy Spirit, and he joins you in power. You can speak the language given to you by the Holy at any time. The more you pray in tongues, the more your language develops. There are many benefits to speaking in tongues. Some of the 60 benefits, described throughout Glenn Arekion's book, *The Power of Praying in Tongues* are as follows:

- Gives a door of utterance, boldness in preaching and teaching
- Speaking reveals divine mysteries, divine coded secrets
- Prophesying your God-ordained future
- Strengthening your inner self with might

- The ignition to walking in the power of God

- Builds and stimulates your faith

- Giving praise and thanksgiving well unto God

- Praying in line with the divine will of God

- Fine-tunes your spirit man to be more sensitive and hear the voice of God

- Helps synchronize us with the timing of God

Glenn Arekion, *The Power of Praying in Tongues*, (San Giovanni Teatino – Italy: Destiny Image Europe, 2010)

The Holy Spirit initiates the gift of tongues. He comes over you and, with your permission, flows powerfully through you. The times he desired to speak through me, I took a breath, and as I released my breath, his tongues flowed out of me just like the scripture says. Out of your belly shall flow rivers of living water. The Word is living water flowing like a mighty river from the throne of God through you. No enemy can withstand the mysteries of the Word released in tongues. In a group setting, someone should receive the interpretation to educate others. If no one comes forward with the understanding, you can ask for it and give it in whatever language is required.

Girting your loins with The Truth is getting ready for spiritual confrontation. This area of the body is also where the scriptures say Jesus was moved with compassion. Compassion coupled with the result of righteous thinking, 'as it should be,' released with what you believe is complete, from your heart, surrounded with the joy of the kingdom of heaven, produces your desire. Jesus was moved with compassion when he saw the multitude full of sick, hungry people, healed the sick, taught them, and fed over ten thousand people. Touching the lepers, he cleansed them with his command. Any type of sickness is a lie. When you release the truth, a lie must leave. There is no sickness in heaven.

With your feet shod with the preparation of the Gospel of Peace, be a peacemaker. Everywhere you go, restore kingdom order by releasing resurrection power in the name of Jesus. Speak to whatever the problem or desire is, telling it what you see. You see what God sees. All things are yours. If the peace of God is not received, move on. Pray always with all prayer and supplication in the Spirit. Use the heavenly language you received from the Holy Spirit. He helps you pray the will of God into your life. After you have prayed in tongues, believe you have received your desire. Praying in tongues also refreshes your spirit. Watch your thoughts and your words after you pray. Stay out of negativity and contention with yourself and others. Most of the time, you have to keep what you have prayed between you and God until it manifests. Protect your environment. Always pray for the people of God earnestly with all persistence.

I Corinthians chapter 12, verses 4 through 11, tell you how the Holy Spirit, Jesus Christ, and God make the spiritual gifts available to you. There are diversities of gifts, but the same Spirit. And there are differences of administrations, but the same Lord. And there are diversities of operations, but it is the same God who works all in all. Operating in the gifts of the Spirit used for knowledge, power, and speaking, are manifestations of the Spirit given to each one to profit with. The gifts used for knowing about something or someone, are the word of wisdom, the word of knowledge, and discerning of spirits. The power gifts are faith, healing, and the working of miracles. The gifts used to speak by the Spirit are the interpretation of tongues, diverse kinds of tongues, and prophecy. Differences in administration use the giving, hospitality, and leadership or governing gifts. Those used for operations are faith and discernment of spirits.

Study the Word with the Holy Spirit. Hear and know the truth. Rest in God, listening, and using the awareness of your senses. Guided by the Holy Spirit, use your spiritual weapons of warfare daily to align encounters with the Word. Watch and pray in the Spirit without ceasing for yourself and others to fight the good fight of faith in Jesus' name.

PART 4: STRATEGIC PREPARATION

Chapter 9

Summary Questions

&

Reference Scriptures

PART 4: STRATEGIC PREPARATION
Chapter 9 Summary Questions

Holy Spirit and the Weapons of Spiritual Warfare
Understanding Their Function and Use

1. How does the Holy Spirit continue the ministry of Jesus Christ?

2. Which piece of armor is the only defensive weapon, and why?

3. What is the importance of imitating God daily?

4. How do you accomplish up to 99% of the decision you make in your spirit?

5. What makes the Lord Jesus Christ the ultimate weapon of Light? Do you agree?

6. How do you allow the strength and power of the Holy Spirit to flow through you?

7. Why should you understand the function and use of your spiritual weapons?

8. Explain the meaning of the two-edged sword and its use.

9. How do the Helmet of Salvation, the Breastplate of Righteousness, moving in compassion in The Truth work together to manifest God's will?

10. How is it possible to pray without ceasing?

Chapter 9 Scripture References
Descriptive Notes Taken from the Scripture for Research

God Created and Made the Heavens and the Earth

Genesis 2:1, 4

Thus the heavens and the earth were finished, and all the host of them. They were created, in the day that the LORD God made the earth and the heavens.

The Holy Spirit Sent to the Earth

John 14:26

But the Comforter, which is the Holy Ghost, whom the Father will send in my name, he shall teach you all things.

John 16:8-11

And when he is come, he will reprove the world of sin, and of righteousness, and of judgment.

Men Loved Darkness

John 3:17-21

And this is the condemnation, that light is come into the world, and men loved darkness rather than light, because their deeds were evil.

Study the Word of God

II Timothy 2:15

Study to shew yourself approved unto God, a workman that needs not to be ashamed, rightly dividing the word of truth.

II Peter 1:19-21
Knowing this first that no prophecy of the scripture is of any private interpretation.

Quickened Together with Christ

Ephesians 2:5-7
Has quickened us together with Christ, raised us up together, and made us sit together in heavenly places in Christ Jesus.

Ephesians 1:17-18
I pray that the God, the Father of glory, give to you the spirit of wisdom and revelation in the knowledge of him. And that the eyes of your understanding be enlightened.

Restoration – The Father's Will

Revelation 5:12
Worthy is the Lamb that was slain to receive power, and riches, and wisdom, and strength, and honor, and glory, and blessing.

Luke 22:42
Saying, Father, if you are willing, remove this cup from me: nevertheless not my will, but yours, be done.

John 12:31
Now is the judgment of this world: now shall the prince of this world be cast out.

Light of the World

John 9:5
As long as I am in the world, I am the light of the world.

Matthew 5:14
You are the light of the world. A city that is set on a hill cannot be hid.

Thoughts and Imagination - Flip the Switch

Genesis 6:5
And God saw that the wickedness of man was great in the earth, and that every imagination of the thoughts of his heart was only evil continually.

II Corinthians 10:5
Casting down imaginations, and every high thing that exalts itself against the knowledge of God.

Isaiah 55:8
For my thoughts are not your thoughts, neither are your ways my ways, says the LORD.

Imitate God

Ephesians 5:1, 8
Follow God as dear children. Walk as children of light.

I Thessalonians 5:5
You are all the children of light, and the children of the day: we are not of the night, nor of darkness.

Live in the Spirit

Galatians 5:25
If we live in the Spirit, let us also walk in the Spirit.

Ephesians 3:20
Now unto him that is able to do exceeding abundantly above all that we ask or think.

Focus, Speak, and Act

Hebrews 12:1-3
Looking unto Jesus the author and finisher of our faith; who for the joy that was set before him endured the cross, despising the shame, and sits at the throne of God.

Angels are on the Earth to Assist You

Psalm 91:11, 14-16
For he shall give his angels charge over you, to keep you in all your ways.

Psalm 103:19-22
You his angels that excel in strength, that do his commandments, hearkening unto the voice of his word. All you his hosts; you ministers of his, that do his pleasure.

Hebrews 1:6-7, 14
Angels of God worship his first begotten. He makes his angels spirits, and his ministers a flame of fire. They are sent forth to minister for them who shall be heirs of salvation?

Fulfill God's Plan for You

Hebrews 10:7
Lo, I come (in the volume of the book it is written of me,) to do your will, O God.

Fasting Keeps You in Control

Acts 14:23
And when they had ordained them elders in every church, and had prayed with fasting, they commended them to the Lord, on whom they believed.

Mark 9:28-29
Why could not we cast him out? He said unto them, this kind can come forth by nothing, but by prayer and fasting.

Be Strong in the Lord

Ephesians 6:10-20
Finally, my brethren, be strong in the Lord, and in the power of his might.

Genesis 1:26-27
And God said, Let us make man in our image, after our likeness: and let them have dominion over all the earth. God created male and female in his own image.

II Corinthians 3:18
We are changed into the same image from glory to glory, by the Spirit of the Lord.

Let Peace Reign

Colossians 3:15
And let the peace of God rule in your hearts, to which also you are called in one body; and be thankful.

Philippians 4:6-7
Don't be anxious for anything. The peace of God, which passes all understanding, shall keep your hearts and minds through Christ Jesus.

The Defeated Devil is Your Adversary

Luke 10:17-19
I beheld Satan as lightning fall from heaven. Behold, I give unto you power to tread on serpents and scorpions, and over all the power of the enemy.

I Peter 5:8-11
Be sober, be vigilant; because your adversary the devil, as a roaring lion, walks about, seeking whom he may devour. Resist steadfast in the faith.

Colossians 2:12-15
And having spoiled principalities and powers, he made a shew of them openly, triumphing over them in it.

Put On the Armor of God

Ephesians 6:11-12
Put on the whole armor of God that you may be able to stand against the wiles of the devil.

Romans 13:11-14
And that, knowing the time, the night is far spent, the day is at hand: let us therefore cast off the works of darkness, put on the armor of light.

Jesus, Far Above All

Ephesians 1:20-23
God set Jesus far above all principality, and power, and might, and dominion, and every name that is named, not only in this world, but also in that which is to come.

Take Unto You the Whole Armor of God

Ephesians 6:13-18
Wherefore take unto you the whole armor of God that you may be able to withstand in the evil day, and having done all, to stand.

Matthew 6:33-34
Seek first the kingdom of God, and his righteousness. Take no thought for tomorrow. Tomorrow will take thought for the things of itself. Sufficient to the day is the evil thereof.

Matthew 6:22-23
The light of the body is the eye: if therefore your eye is single, your whole body shall be full of light. But if your eye is evil, your whole body shall be full of darkness.

Habakkuk 3:4
And his brightness was as the light; he had horns coming out of his hand: and there was the hiding of his power.

I Timothy 6:12
Fight the good fight of faith, lay hold on eternal life, whereunto you are also called, and have professed a good profession before many witnesses.

The Gift of Righteousness

Romans 5:17-21
By one man's offence death reigned by one; much more they which receive abundance of grace and of the gift of righteousness shall reign in life by one, Jesus Christ.

II Timothy 2:22
Follow righteousness, faith, love, peace, with them that call on the Lord out of a pure heart.

Issues Life with Your Heart

Proverbs 4:20-24
Keep your heart with all diligence; for out of it are the issues of life.

Colossians 3:16-17
Let the word of Christ dwell in you richly in all wisdom; teaching and admonishing one another in song. Sing with grace in your hearts to the Lord.

Ephesians 3:16-19
That Christ may dwell in your hearts by faith. Be rooted and grounded in love. Understand and know the love of Christ to be filled with all the fullness of God.

The Fruit of Righteousness

James 3:17-18
And the fruit of righteousness is sown in peace of them that make peace.

Philippians 1:9-11
Being filled with the fruits of righteousness, which are by Jesus Christ, unto the glory and praise of God.

The Helmet of Salvation

I Thessalonians 5:8
But let us, who are of the day, be sober, putting on the breastplate of faith and love; and for a helmet, the hope of salvation.

Romans 12:1-2
Be not conformed to this world: but be you transformed by the renewing of your mind.

Ephesians 4:23
And be renewed in the spirit of your mind.

Power, Love and a Sound Mind

II Timothy 1:7
God has not given us the spirit of fear; but of power, and of love, and of a sound mind.

I John 4:16-18
There is no fear in love; but perfect love casts out fear.

Sweet Smelling Savor

Ephesians 5:2
And walk in love, as Christ also hath loved us, and hath given himself for us an offering and a sacrifice to God for a sweet smelling savor.

A Man's Belly

Proverbs 18:20-21
A man's belly shall be satisfied with the fruit of his mouth; and with the increase of his lips shall he be filled. Death and life are in the power of the tongue.

Proverbs 6:2
Thou art snared with the words of your mouth, thou art taken with the words of your mouth.

Meditate with the Holy Spirit

Psalm 19:14
Let the words of my mouth, and the meditation of my heart, be acceptable in your sight.

Psalm 39:1-3
My heart was hot within me, while I was musing the fire burned: then I spoke.

Two-Edged Sword

Hebrews 4:12
For the word of God is quick, and powerful, and sharper than any two edged sword.

Hebrews 1:3
Who being the brightness of his glory, the express image of his person, and upholding all things by the word of his power, purged our sins.

Revelation 1:16

He had in his right hand seven stars. Out of his mouth went a sharp two edged sword.

Girt Your Loins - The Truth - Compassion

Isaiah 11:4-5

And righteousness shall be the girdle of his loins, and faithfulness the girdle of his reins.

Matthew 14:14-21

And Jesus went forth, and saw a great multitude, and was moved with compassion toward them, and he healed their sick.

The Gospel of Peace

Matthew 5:9

Blessed are the peacemakers: for they shall be called the children of God.

The Holy Spirit Intercedes For Us

Romans 8:26-27

The Spirit makes intercession for the saints according to the will of God.

The Gifts of the Holy Spirit

I Corinthians 12:4-11

There are diversities of gifts, but the same Spirit; differences of administrations, but the same Lord; diversities of operations, but it is the same God which works all in all.

John 7:37-39
He that believeth on me, out of his belly shall flow rivers of living water.

I Thessalonians 5:17
Pray without ceasing.

CHAPTER 10

Moving By Holy Spirit Instructions

Recognizing Problems, Overcoming Obstacles, Obtaining Promises

The Holy Spirit is ready for Gem to experience his power. "Gem," he asks, "are you ready to use what you have learned to change lives?" Gem has come a long way from being controlled like a puppet in dirty clothes to wearing God's powerful armor in Christ. To war a good warfare in the wilderness of the world system, while maintaining the power of his Godhead alignment in spirit, soul, and body, he must hear in the spirit, use his senses, and move by the Holy Spirit's voice. With heartfelt determination, he responds, "Yes, Holy Spirit, I'm ready. I'll follow you wherever you lead me!"

The Holy Spirit teaches you how to live in God's glory, releasing his resurrection power to change what others think is unchangeable. Directed by the Holy Spirit, recognize problems, overcome obstacles, and obtain the promises with the assistance of God's heavenly host. Receive The Blessing of the New Covenant by faith. Know that all the promises in Jesus Christ are not yes and no, but yes, and in him, amen.

In the first part of Isaiah's prophecy, chapter 61, verse 1 describes the ministry of Jesus Christ. He says, 'The Spirit of the Lord GOD is upon me because the LORD has anointed me to preach good tidings unto the meek. He has sent me to bind up the brokenhearted, to proclaim liberty to the captives, and the opening of the prison to them that are bound. He has sent me to proclaim the acceptable year of the LORD, and the day of vengeance of our God. To comfort all that mourn.'

Jesus reads the account of Isaiah's prophecy about himself in Luke chapter 4, verses 18 and 19, ending with 'To proclaim the acceptable year of the Lord.' He closes the book, gives it to the minister, and sits down. With everyone in the synagogue still staring at him, he says, 'This day is this scripture fulfilled in your ears.' During his ministry, anointed by the Holy Spirit, Jesus Christ preached the goodness of God, healed and restored hearts, proclaimed freedom from oppression, and opened the doors of captivity so the spiritually blind through unbelief could set themselves free. He did not read, 'the day of vengeance of our God; to comfort all that mourn.' 'The day of vengeance of our God' was not part of his assignment. The Lord Jesus Christ is the head of the body, the church. As a member of his body, the last part of his prophecy is your assignment. It is called the ministry of reconciliation.

Going back to Isaiah chapter 61, in verse 4, the prophecy continues by describing the condition of the people before and after the resurrection. The ministry of Jesus freed the people and provided the Shalom of salvation. Remember, Shalom, means completeness, wholeness, health, peace, welfare, safety, soundness, tranquility, prosperity, perfectness, fullness, rest, harmony, and the absence of agitation or discord. The root verb means to be complete, perfect, and full. Now, you are living in the day of vengeance of our God. In the name of Jesus, moving by the Holy Spirit's instructions, you are here to comfort all that mourn. The kingdom of God is righteousness, peace, and joy. Appoint to them that mourn in Zion, beauty for ashes, the oil of joy for mourning, and the garment of praise for the spirit of heaviness. In beauty, joy, and praise, they are called trees of righteousness, the planting of the LORD, that he may be glorified. Then, together as trees of righteousness, build the old wastes. Raise up the former desolations, and repair the waste cities, the desolations of many generations.

The disciples, who sadly returned to their past lives after the crucifixion, now baptized by the Holy Spirit, and dedicated wholly to serving the Lord, preached everywhere demonstrating the resurrection of Jesus Christ with signs following. What changed them? Entering through the veil of the Holy of Holies by the Blood of Jesus, they became true worshippers of the Father in spirit and truth. Then stepping out boldly as warriors who worship God in the Lord Jesus Christ, they allow the Holy Spirit to lead in all their decisions. To carry out the vengeance of the LORD against the enemy and repair the waste places, they had to follow the Holy Spirit, who knows the deep things of God.

Live your life as a Worship Warrior. Become skilled in living eternal life from your spirit man in the NOW, unto God your Father. Live and walk in the spirit actively wearing and moving forward in the Armor of Light. Welcome the Holy Spirit to flow within you yielding to and resting in the presence of God. As the flow of the Spirit increases within you, allow the Holy Spirit to manifest his fruit in you, work his gifts through you, as you flow in wisdom, knowledge, counsel, might, understanding, and the fear of the LORD.

You are the temple of the Holy Spirit. As a warrior who worships God before you start your day, and in all you think, say, and do, you remain who you are in Christ, no matter what life presents. Offering your life as worship to the Father is your highest priority. Receive the will of God, and the strategy to carry it out in yourself first, and then on the earth by the Holy Spirit's leading. He knows that the reality of heaven must manifest in your life before you can fill the earth with the knowledge of the glory of the LORD.

Jesus willingly took all sin on the cross, giving his life to redeem humanity and reconcile all things by his resurrection. You as a warrior who worships your Father in heaven, have embraced the doing of his will. Resting in him, allows the release of his power through you by faith in his name and enables you to live, move, and have your being with Christ in God. Release God's proceeding Word on the earth as your own. The zeal of the LORD of hosts performs the Word you speak. Knowing that you have the keys of the Kingdom of Heaven to bind and loose his will, retain and remit sin, and to open doors and shut doors in heaven and on the earth, you expect to see the works and the fulfillment of God's will in the NOW of his presence.

Apostle Paul's mindset after his Damascus road experience with Jesus Christ changed from the righteousness of the law, to fulfill the righteousness that is through the faith of Jesus Christ and of God. He desired to know the person of Christ, and experience the power of his resurrection. Looking forward, Paul wanted to make his inner man conform to the likeness of Jesus Christ, his sufferings, and even to his death. Paul indeed worshipped God as a warrior, as he pressed toward the mark for the prize of the high calling of God in Christ Jesus.

Paul moved by the Holy Spirit to recognize problems, overcome obstacles, and obtain promises throughout his ministry. In Roman chapter 8, verses 35 and 37 through 39 say, 'Who shall separate us from the love of Christ? Shall tribulation, or distress, or persecution, or famine, or nakedness, or peril, or sword? In all these things, we are more than conquerors through him that loved us. For I am persuaded, that neither death, nor life, nor angels, nor principalities, nor powers, nor things present, nor things to come, nor height, nor depth, nor any other creature, shall be able to separate us from the love of God, which is in Christ Jesus our Lord.'

Just like Jesus Christ, the disciples, and Paul, you have 'Now' authority with no waiting. Maintain a listening ear with availability for an on-going conversation with the Holy Spirit. Your capacity to hear and follow the Holy Spirit is evidence of the maturity and ability of your spiritual senses. The Lord confirms the Word you speak with signs, miracles, deliverance, and healings following you. Pursue, overtake, and recover all in the wilderness of the world by following the Holy Spirit's commands and timing. Use your spiritual senses to hear, see, and know that whatever you are pursuing is already done.

The following are just a few of the many experiences I've had in my life with the Holy Spirit. Many, many other spiritual encounters described in my autobiography book, "Daddy's Little Girl," have taught me how to live from the spiritual realm. The ups and downs of my life show you that because you trust God, no matter what happens, he will use you to obtain his promises for yourself and others.

Move Over!

There were times in my life when the Holy Spirit would show me situations before they happened. Usually, within three days from the time the Holy Spirit showed me a particular situation, a person's face, or a name whatever it was would take place. Sometimes I would hear the entire conversation with the person in the spirit ahead of time. Once I heard or saw a situation in the spirit, I would wait expecting it to come to pass.

Most of the time, an event would happen within three days, but sometimes it would happen in seconds or minutes. I would run into the person and have the entire conversation just as I had heard it, word for word. Waiting for them to say what I had heard in my spirit before that moment, I would answer them with what I already knew to say. For years, it was always within three days. I found these times to be very inspiring.

One particular day in California, I was driving down Interstate 5 South just past the Coronado Bridge. Back then, I use to drive a yellow '72 Volkswagen Bug. All of a sudden, the Holy Spirit said, "Look in the rearview mirror!"

Looking in the mirror, I saw a woman probably in her 40's, driving right behind me in my lane. She was screaming and had a terrified look on her face. Her hair was all messy and sticking up in an angle like she was blowing away. Her face looked contorted in terror and awful pain.

I turned around quickly and looked over my right shoulder into the lane behind me. There indeed was a woman driving, but her face looked normal to me. I turned around, wondering what it was all about. About 3 to 4 seconds after I turned back around to continue driving, the Holy Spirit said very urgently, "Move over!"

Immediately, I looked to my left to make sure the lane was clear and moved over. In less than 3 seconds, a car sped down the ramp onto the freeway at a very high rate of speed and crossed diagonally over 3 of the lanes of traffic hitting the back end of the woman's car. The impact pushed her forward parallel with my car and then spun her around several times. Cars behind her began hitting her and piling up. As I looked in the rearview mirror, I saw the pile-up and the woman screaming just as the Holy Spirit had shown me.

If I had not obeyed the Holy Spirit and had stayed in the lane, I would have been in the middle of the multi-car pile-up and certainly would have been seriously injured if not worse.

'Knife' At My Throat

Some years ago, God trusted me and possibly others by warning me ahead of time that there would be a knife attack on someone. At that time, I was living in California and worked in a central office building downtown on 9th and C Streets. As usual, after work, I walked alone for several blocks to the parking lot where I parked my car. As I reached my yellow '72 VW Bug, I opened the door and sat down behind the wheel.

Immediately, I felt a quick slice from the edge of a knife across my throat. It was a very definite swipe, but it felt as light as a feather. It startled me for a moment, then realizing that no one was in the car with me, I waited to see if a bad feeling or a dark feeling would immediately accompany what had just happened. There was no bad feeling that came over me, so I knew that it was meant for someone else.

At first, I thought of family members and asked God to protect them, but the Holy Spirit didn't give me a witness in my spirit that a family member was in danger. As I listened so I would know what to do, I didn't hear anything from the Holy Spirit, so I prayed for the person who the warning was for, that the angels would protect them.

I thought that would be the end of it, but the next day after work I walked to my car, opened the door and sat down. The exact same thing with the knife slice happened again right across my throat. I really paid attention then, and again I listened to hear something from the Holy Spirit. Again, I heard nothing. The next day, the same thing happened again. I felt the slice across my throat three days in a row.

It just so happened that the small church I attended at that time had service on Wednesday nights and praise God, it was Wednesday. During testimony service, I stood up and told the people about what I had experienced in the car. I didn't know if they would believe me, but a person's life was at stake. I told them that I had prayed for the person, but I would like for all of us to pray and agree that God would protect whoever the person. Of course, we prayed.

On television, two days later, the news reported that a woman who ran a mission downtown was attacked on the sidewalk by a man with a knife. He had grabbed her from behind and held a knife to her throat. People on the street saw the whole thing.

Witnesses said that as he threatened her, he began to shake violently, dropped the knife, and ran away. God spared the woman's life, and she was unharmed. Praise our Father God for his love, his warning, and his excellent protection. Agreement with God in prayer works every time.

God Made My Payment

We were in so much debt that I was 'robbing Peter to pay Paul' every month just to make the minimum payments on bills. I would make a payment on a loan at the Credit Union, wait for it to post, and then transfer the available balance to pay another bill, or to have enough for gas or food. I knew this was not God's will, and the guilt I carried for allowing myself to be put in this situation was tremendous. Nevertheless, I knew that God could do the impossible if I would just trust him for it.

Santeller was an automated machine at the Credit Union that we referred to as the Iron Lady. You called Santeller with your account number and access codes to check your account balances, the due dates of payments, to make payments, etc. While working at "C" Street in the central office, I believed that if I called Santeller, God would make my payment for me. The technology was his. He made the computers, so when I inquired about my monthly loan payment, he could undoubtedly override the electronic Iron Lady and make her say, 'Paid.' Then I wouldn't have to make the loan payment just to borrow it back. I could use the cash to pay another bill and stop the borrowing. In this way, I could eventually pay the loan off.

I made that decision and then walked down one of the rows of equipment to pray. I asked God to make the payment for me. I thanked him for it and headed toward the panel where the telephone was. I stood there a few seconds looking at the receiver and then picked it up and made the call. Somehow, I felt that all of heaven was watching me. I dialed the required digits, fully expecting the machine to say, "Paid." When Santeller said,

"Paid!" it startled me, but praise God! With man it is impossible, but with God all things are possible!

All 3 Bones in My Ankle Healed

I broke my ankle when I was 38 years old. I fell while playing a roller rink game of tag on roller skates and broke all three bones in my ankle. That was a shame because I was one of about 7 or 8 people left who hadn't been tagged yet. My husband asked me if I wanted us to pray for healing, or if I wanted him to take me to the hospital Emergency. My ankle was swelling very quickly, so I told him to take me to the hospital. The technician took x-rays of my broken ankle, and then took me to another room for an attendant to set it in a cast.

All three of the bones in my ankle were broken. As I waited, I wondered if I had to get a shot. Immediately, I saw a large syringe out in front of me in the spirit realm. I said to myself out loud, "I don't want to get a shot!" Just then, the attendant came into the room and said, "It's been ten years since you've had a tetanus shot, so yes, you have to get a shot." I don't know who he thought I was talking to before he came in, because I was the only person in the room.

He gave me the shot and then prepared the materials needed to set my leg. He told me that he couldn't give me anything for pain. I said in a low voice, "God, you know I don't like pain." I was sitting on an examination table. He brought a small stool over to sit on, smiled at me apologetically and said, "Now this is going to hurt." He took ahold of my ankle, then pushed and pressed the bones into place. Miraculously, there was no pain. He kept looking up at me, puzzled, expecting me to cry out in pain, but I didn't God had taken the pain.

After he put a temporary cast on me from the knee down, I left on crutches with the x-ray, and instructions to have my doctor in San Diego check my ankle. My doctor had another x-ray taken, and then hung the two of them up for comparison. In the first x-ray, all three of my ankle bones were broken. In the x-ray he had taken, all three ankle bones were normal. As I watched him expecting to see a reaction, his neck jerked from one x-ray to the other in disbelief. I looked at him calmly. He realized that God had intervened and healed me.

He asked me to walk carefully across the small examination room. He said that I could walk well in the cast, but just to make sure, he wanted to put a full cast on my leg and leave it on for six weeks. That meant I had to stay home in a wheelchair. I didn't like it because I knew that God healed my ankle in the emergency room, but I did it.

Pain in My Leg Healed

A couple of months before my husband and I were married, I began to have pain in my right leg. I used my faith by listening to teachings on healing, reading healing scriptures, praying, commanding, and using visualization to see Jesus take my pain on the cross. Nothing seemed to work. As time passed by, the pain only grew worse.

I had been to Urgent Care, insisting that they order X-rays. The doctor didn't see anything in the X-rays. He asked me if I had played sports when I was younger, and I told him that I had. He chalked the pain up to old age and told me to take pain medicine every day. He also stated that I would probably have to take it for the rest of my life. Well, those were fighting words because I was not going to be in pain for the rest of my life, and the last thing I wanted to do was get in the habit of taking pain killers!

Righteous indignation rose up in me, and I told him that I intended to do nothing of the sort. Each day, when the muscle in my leg warmed up from walking, I didn't feel the pain, but in the morning after sleeping all night, or if I sat too long, as soon as I moved, the pain would hit me. I was determined not to take any medicine unless the pain became unbearable, and I didn't.

The pain was in my head and my heart. I knew it was a lie and that healing was already mine, but I couldn't shake it. My husband had to help me put my shoe on my right foot because I couldn't raise my leg high enough to put on a sock or shoe. Getting dressed was very difficult because I had trouble reaching down on the right side without pain hitting me. I had been in pain now for a year and a half. Something had to be done about it.

I had to depend on the healing power of the word of God. I knew the glory of God was in me. I just had to learn how to get it to flow through my leg. I asked the Holy Spirit how to make that happen. My faith and everything I had learned was not working. The pain was in control and not the power of the Holy Spirit. Over time, he asked me a question, and later, he directed me to the scripture. He asked, "If your finger didn't hurt, would you think about it?" Then, he said, "When the Word gets louder than the pain, you'll be healed." He did this to help me change my thinking as I endured the pain while believing I was already healed. He told me to put myself in **Hebrews 12:2**.

> **Hebrews 12:2** *Looking unto Jesus the author and finisher of our faith; who for the joy that was set before him endured the cross, despising the shame, and is set down at the right hand of the throne of God.*

> **Hebrews 12:2** *Looking unto Jesus the author and finisher of* **(my)** *faith; who for the* **(healing)** *that* **(is)** *set before* **(me)** *endured the* **(hurt muscle)***, despising the* **(pain)***, and* **(I am)** *set down at the right hand of the throne of God* **(with/in him)** *healed.*

I had to see and count myself as healed now. It didn't matter if the pain roared at me. In the morning, when I woke up, I couldn't allow myself to think the thought, 'If I move my leg, it will hurt.' I had to get to the point that my thoughts and words agreed with II Peter 2:24, which says by whose stripes you were healed.

If I count this scripture as real in me, then there is no way I would ever have that thought or say those words. Finally, I mastered it and came up over the pain with my thoughts, words and actions. Soon after, I was sitting on the bench at the end of our bed. I put my left leg up on my right leg and put my sock on. Immediately, the Holy Spirit said, "Put the other leg up there." I almost had the thought that I couldn't do that, but praise God; I did not think that thought! I put my right leg up on my left leg, and it didn't hurt! I shouted, "It didn't hurt!" I have not had any pain in my right leg since that day.

PART 4: STRATEGIC PREPARATION

Chapter 10

Summary Questions
&
Reference Scriptures

PART 4: STRATEGIC PREPARATION
Chapter 10 Summary Questions

Moving By Holy Spirit Instructions
Recognizing Problems, Overcoming Obstacles, Obtaining Promises

1. Describe one problem that you once thought could not be changed. What is the obstacle facing you that you need to overcome to obtain your promise?

2. Do you understand Isaiah chapter 61, verse 2? What is your area of assignment concerning verse 2b?

3. What were some of the undesirable conditions the people were subject to in Luke chapter 4, verse 18 that continue to control people today? Why?

4. What is a Worship Warrior?

5. How do you increase your spiritual capacity so the Holy Spirit can increase the manifestation of his fruit, gifts, and spiritual flow through you?

6. Why is God's strategy for your day so important?

7. Why is it vital for you, the temple of the Holy Spirit, to worship at the throne of God in his temple?

8. What is the benefit of believing in God's love for you?

9. How do you know what God has given you is already yours?

10. Why does your 'Now' authority in Jesus' name come with no waiting?

Chapter 10 Scripture References
Descriptive Notes Taken from the Scripture for Research

War a Good Warfare

I Timothy 1:18-19
According to the prophecies which went before on you, by them war a good warfare; holding faith, and a good conscience.

The Promises of God in Jesus Are Yes

II Corinthians 1:19-20
For the Son of God, Jesus Christ was not yes and no, but in him was yes. For all the promises of God in him are yes, and in him Amen, unto the glory of God by us.

The Acceptable Year of the LORD

Isaiah 61:1-2
The Spirit of the Lord GOD is upon me. He has anointed me to proclaim the acceptable year of the LORD, and the day of vengeance of our God; to comfort all that mourn.

Luke 4:18-21
The Spirit of the Lord is upon me, because he hath anointed me to preach the acceptable year of the Lord. He said, 'This day is this scripture fulfilled in your ears.'

I Corinthians 6:15, 17
Know you not that your bodies are the members of Christ? But he that is joined unto the Lord is one spirit.

The Ministry of Reconciliation

II Corinthians 5:18
And all things are of God, who hath reconciled us to himself by Jesus Christ, and hath given to us the ministry of reconciliation.

Isaiah 61:3-4
To appoint unto them that mourn in Zion, to give unto them beauty for ashes, the oil of joy for mourning, the garment of praise for the spirit of heaviness.

Isaiah 59:14-21
For he put on righteousness as a breastplate, and a helmet of salvation upon his head; and he put on the garments of vengeance for clothing, and was clad with zeal as a cloak.

Worship Warrior

Acts 1:13-15
They went up into an upper room, these all continued with one accord in prayer and supplication, with the women, and Mary the mother of Jesus, and with his brethren.

Mark 16:20
And they went forth, and preached everywhere, the Lord working with them, and confirming the word with signs following. Amen.

Hebrews 10:19-22
Having boldness to enter into the holiest by the blood of Jesus, by a new and living way, which he hath consecrated for us, through the veil, that is to say, his flesh.

Matthew 6:9-10
Our Father which art in heaven, Hallowed be your name. Your kingdom come. Your will be done in earth, as it is in heaven.

John 4:23-24
But the hour cometh, and now is, when the true worshippers shall worship the Father in spirit and in truth: for the Father seeks such to worship him.

I John 1:3
Have fellowship with us. Truly our fellowship is with the Father, and with his Son Jesus Christ.

Habakkuk 2:14
For the earth shall be filled with the knowledge of the glory of the LORD, as the waters cover the sea.

John 4:34
Jesus said to them, 'My meat is to do the will of him that sent me, and to finish his work.'

The Release of God's Power

Habakkuk 3:4
And his brightness was as the light; he had horns coming out of his hand: and there was the hiding of his power.

The Keys

Matthew 16:19
With the keys of the kingdom of heaven, whatsoever you shall bind on earth shall be bound in heaven: and whatsoever you shall loose on earth shall be loosed in heaven.

John 20:21-23
Receive the Holy Ghost. Who's so ever sins you remit, they are remitted unto them; and who's so ever sins you retain; they are retained.

Matthew 18:18-20
If two of you shall agree on earth as touching anything that they shall ask, it shall be done for them of my Father which is in heaven. There am I in the midst of them.

Revelation 1:18
I am he that lives, and was dead; and, behold, I am alive for ever-more, Amen; and have the keys of hell and of death.

Revelation 3:7
These things say he that is holy, he that is true, he that hath the key of David, he that opens, and no man shuts; and shuts, and no man opens.

The Apostle Paul Called to Ministry

Acts 26:9-20
Delivering you from the people, and from the Gentiles, to whom now I send you, to open their eyes, to turn them from darkness to light, and from the power of Satan to God.

Philippians 3:7-8
But what things were gain to me, those I counted loss for Christ. Yes doubtless, and I count all things but loss for the excellency of the knowledge of Christ Jesus my Lord.

Philippians 3:9
And be found in him, not having mine own righteousness, which is of the law, but that which is through the faith of Christ, the righteousness which is of God by faith.

Philippians 3:10-12

That I may know him, and the power of his resurrection, and the fellowship of his sufferings, being made conformable unto his death.

Romans 8:28-39

In all these things we are more than conquerors through him that loved us.

Maintain a Listening Ear

I John 2:20

But you have an unction from the Holy One, and you know all things.

Pursue, Overtake and Recover All

I Samuel 30:1-8

David enquired at the LORD, Shall I pursue after this troop? Shall I overtake them? He answered him, Pursue: for you shall surely overtake them, and without fail recover all.

PART 5: THE KINGDOM LIFESTYLE

Preeminence

CHAPTER 11

Living Life in the Kingdom
The Challenge of Living in Two Realms

Before Gem can face his oppressor and exercise dominion over the negative influence of the world system, he must face himself. The open doors of condemnation, fear, and stress that allowed the puppet master to overwhelm and control him in the past, are now closed. Gem must enforce their closures by meeting every opportunity knowing that his conscience, having been sprinkled with the Blood of Jesus, is no longer subject to his enemy. Gem, with no thought or sense of condemnation, must confront him, or counter his attacks with the power of the Word and demonstration on every level. Protecting his heavenly atmosphere, environment, and surroundings is paramount to maintaining his ability to hear, understand, and execute the Holy Spirit's instructions.

Gem begins his conversation with the Holy Spirit by saying, "I see my life differently now that I've learned so much from you.

I feel more confident here in heaven's realm on earth. Facing the same people in my family, the neighborhood, at church, even at the grocery store will feel different for me. I know how to listen and hear you. You are there with me, even now, telling me what to say before someone asks me how my appearance has changed so. They can see my face when I walk. My chin is up, and my shoulders are straight. I walk tall like I'm going somewhere. No one is making me do anything. I can feel the look of confidence on my face and in my heart. My mind is clear, and my spirit is ready. I expect to experience the goodness of God." The Holy Spirit's response is short and to the point. "We've made you so. Shield up, soldier. Believe only. Speak the Word only."

Learning to live eternal life, simultaneously in two realms, is challenging and exciting. Dwelling in the present, in the surrounding presence of the 'Supreme One,' Elohim, means living in perfect alignment with the sovereignty of the Godhead. Spiritual awareness, freedom, and transformation have renewed your mindset allowing you to rest in his ability. Now, everything in life has potentially changed for you. Being consciously aware of your spiritual alignment with Elohim, God the Father, God the Son, and God the Holy Spirit, and your relationship with each of them allows his power to flow into you, through you, and around you. As an ambassador on earth from the kingdom of heaven, you now live with ease in heaven's atmosphere, environment, and surroundings both in the heavenly and earthly realms.

How is this possible? You are a king and a priest, a member of the resurrected body of Christ. The fullness of the Godhead dwells in him wholly. Jesus Christ spoiled, that is put off and disarmed, principalities and powers, showing their weaknesses openly by triumphing over them. He is the head of all principality and power, and you are complete in him. Buried with Jesus Christ in baptism, you have risen with him through the faith of God from the dead. Putting off the body of the sins of the flesh by the circumcision of Christ, God has forgiven you all trespasses and quickened you together with Christ. The Godhead is in you because you are in the resurrected Christ. He is your example of how to live in God's presence while receiving and releasing the wisdom, power, and glory of God. In his kingdom, the miraculous realm of heaven on earth, you live and walk in the Spirit, recognizing the light of God's presence in and around you.

The following explanation of I Peter chapter 2, verse 9, only touches the surface of who you are, what you have, and what you can do in the resurrected Lord Jesus Christ. As a child or mature son of God, you have been reborn into the chosen forty-second generation of the Son of man. You are children of light, the truth, and its knowledge. Stay calm and collected in spirit, faith, and love because you are children of the day, the last day of this present age. God has made you a priest in his royal priesthood. As a priest in Christ, go to the throne of grace without condemnation to obtain mercy and help for yourself and others in times of need. Purchased by the Blood of Jesus, you are God's possession in a holy nation. He is the one who called you out of darkness into his marvelous light. Because of who God is, and all the good he does for you, praise him openly in all you say and do.

Revelation chapter 5, verse 12, tells us that after his ascension, the Lord Jesus Christ received power, riches, wisdom, strength, honor, glory, and blessing. Because you are a joint-heir with him, so did you. To be an effective ambassador for Christ, learn about each of them from the Holy Spirit, and incorporate them into your life from God's perspective. He will develop the maturity of your awareness and authority in each area by helping you to apply them to your daily life. With the Holy Spirit, learn, implement, and experience their use in your life before he sends you to people in the world system. By taking the time to accomplish this, you will mature and develop personally in their knowledge and the strategy for their use. With the knowledge and understanding of God's will working through you, you will achieve on-going success in your life.

Power, listed first in Revelation chapter 5, verse 12, has several meanings, including strength, force, ability, and dominion. By faith, release the power of God residing in you to perform miracles in Jesus' name. The Holy Spirit will identify areas in your soul and body that need healing. Release his glorious healing power within creating an avenue for moral excellence in every part of your soul. Your soul, healed from condemnation, fear, and stress, will heal your body.

Riches is the fullness and abundance of internal and external possessions. Wealth and riches give you power and influence. I Timothy chapter 6, verses 17 and 18, tell you not to be high-minded or trust in money or possessions, but trust in the living God who gives you richly all things to enjoy. Enriched by the money and wealth God has blessed you with, you are to do good, be rich in good works, ready to distribute, and be willing to give freely. The power and influence of riches also mean an abundance of resources, or the power and influence resting upon armies, forces, and hosts. All of heaven, including God's angels, his heavenly hosts, follow his commands concerning you. The angels obey the Word of God you speak. As you can see, God's power flowing spiritually and naturally is defined and used differently in both realms.

Wisdom, the supreme intelligence of God, used in very diverse matters, is available to us. The eternal power and Godhead are expressed clearly by the invisible things God has made from the creation of the world. The wisdom of God is evident in forming and executing counsels in the formation and government of the world. All wisdom in scripture is the inspiration of God and is profitable for doctrine, reproof, correction, and instruction in righteousness. You cannot know God by using your wisdom. Preach the Word in the power of God's wisdom and not by man's wisdom. Proverbs Chapter 4, verse 7, says, Wisdom is the principal thing; therefore get wisdom: and with all your getting get understanding.

Strength is ability, force, and might. Minister with the ability God gives you, so he is glorified through Jesus Christ. He has made you a king. The king shall joy in the strength of the LORD because his joy is your strength. Standing in his presence, submit to, receive, and be strengthened with all might according to his glorious power unto all patience and endurance with joyfulness.

By the sacrifice of Jesus Christ, the New Covenant in his Blood came into force after his death. Without the death of the testator, the New Covenant would have no strength. Rejoice in the presence of God to refresh and strengthen your spirit.

Show honor to one of dignity who is primarily of the highest degree. It is precious and comes bestowed with a price. The Father crowned Jesus with glory and honor because, by grace, he would taste death for everyone. Let the trial of your faith, which is more precious than gold, be found unto praise, honor, and glory at the appearing of Jesus Christ. God has called you unto his eternal glory by Christ Jesus by grace. Let him make you perfect, establish, strengthen, and settle you. To him be glory and dominion forever.

Glory is opinion, judgment, and view. In the New Covenant, glory is always a good opinion concerning you, resulting in praise, and honor. It is also magnificence, excellence, preeminence, dignity, and grace. Glory is the supreme majesty which belongs to God as supreme ruler, and sovereignty in the sense of the absolute perfection of deity. Glory is apparent in his splendor and the view of his exterior brightness. It is the kingly majesty of the Messiah, the Christ, and his most glorious condition with God the Father in heaven to which he ascended after his resurrection. God, being able to keep you from falling, presents you without blame before the presence of his glory with exceeding joy. You are a mighty king. Give God glory for who he is, strength for what he does, and the glory that is due to his name. Worship him the beauty of holiness. To God, be glory and majesty, dominion and power, both now and forever.

Charge your atmosphere with thanks and praise to the Lord. With grace in your heart, sing a new song to the Lord. Bless his name, his power, and his salvation. The Lord God is great. His greatness is unsearchable. Outwardly praise him, representing him, with all you do and say each day. Praise his works to the next generation, and declare his mighty acts. He is good to all, and his tender mercies are over all his works. Bless the Lamb who redeemed and sanctified the lost to God by his Blood out of every kindred, tongue, people, and nation. He declares God's name to you in the midst of you, the church, and sings praise to God. Believe in, love, and honor the Lamb rejoicing with joy, unspeakable, and full of glory. Be filled with the Spirit, speaking to yourselves in psalms, hymns, and spiritual songs, singing and making melody in your heart to the Lord.

Jesus Christ, who lived his life simultaneously in two realms in worship and obedience to his Father, is your example of victorious living. No matter what was happening around him, he maintained his focus, hearing directly from the Holy Spirit, and acting or speaking what he saw and heard. With no sense of lack, he fulfilled his purpose in life and ministry. To replace what needs to change in the earth realm, set your desires on things above. As an ambassador for Christ, seek the kingdom of God first and his righteousness.

Ask the Holy Spirit for the proceeding Word of God, scripture, or scriptures to plant in your heart. With the joy of the Lord, creating inspiration and strength, believe it, and speak it into your heart. Meditate on the Word you've planted with the Holy Spirit, protecting it from a lack of understanding and shallow roots. By taking action in your spirit, you prevent the rise of tribulation and persecution because of the Word you've received in your heart from causing offense in you. Knowing that you have what you have planted, disarms the cares of the world and the deceitfulness of riches that come to choke the Word growing in you. If you allow the ways of the world into your heart, they will cause the Word to become unfruitful.

You are a king, a priest, and a Worship Warrior Ambassador who maintains victory in your atmosphere, environment, and surroundings. In Jesus Christ, you are one with God whose spoken Word is past tense. With the understanding you have received from the Holy Spirit, bear the fruit of the Word by letting it bud within your spirit. Watch for spiritual signs and visions, and listen to hear from the Holy Spirit. Follow him to bring forth your desire, with disciple and focus. If you have questions, ask him, and he will answer you. In your imagination, step into the result, and live there in the 'now.' Guard your God-given thoughts and joyful emotions. Throughout the day, only think in line with your new position. Only allow the feelings and emotions of your manifested desire by living from it in the present tense. Let negative thoughts float away, refusing to think them. Remember, God is. With gratitude and praise, give God thanks each day.

Because you think and see the result, consistently speaking words of life into it, cultivates and strengthens it, allowing it to manifest spiritual and natural provision in and around you. Protecting your God-given areas of influence maintains growth, as you increase, direct, and flow, moving your momentum in the right direction. Speaking in tongues is an act of worship to God, and it's warfare that keeps your spirit, soul, and body fit for life and service. Worship in song, dance, and the Word of your power with God's thinking, believing, speaking, and actions.

From your heart, minister reconciliation to humanity through Jesus Christ. By faith, release the atmosphere, environment, and surroundings of the kingdom, power, and glory of God within you to the people in the world. With the Holy Spirit's help, see all people through God's heart perspective, and his perception. Jesus said, 'Believe on me to do the same works I do. You shall do greater works than these because I go to my Father. And whatsoever you shall ask in my name, that will I do, that the Father may be glorified in the Son.' Doing greater works means bridging the gap between the kingdom of God within you and the kingdoms of the world system by lighting the way to the eternal love and life of God.

PART 5: THE KINGDOM LIFESTYLE

Chapter 11

Summary Questions
&
Reference Scriptures

PART 5: THE KINGDOM LIFESTYLE
Chapter 11 Summary Questions

Living Life in the Kingdom
The Challenge of Living in Two Realms

1. What is the deepest root the enemy uses to build control of your conscience?

2. Why are you no longer subject to his devices and suggestions?

3. How does standing on earth, in perfect alignment with the heavenly realm in you, change your perspective, strategy, authority, and way of living?

4. Who are you in Christ? Have you received what you have in him, and what can you do as a joint-heir with him?

5. How do you maintain, distribute, and increase wealth and riches?

6. Does your life honor God, and how?

7. As an ambassador for the Lord Jesus Christ, why is your expression of praise, joy, and blessing so essential to maintaining your atmosphere, environment, and surroundings?

8. How does your garden grow? What is your part from the time you plant the Word in your heart?

9. Who brings it forth, you, or God?

10. Why do you view and act on the past tense of God's spoken Word?

Chapter 11 Scripture References
Descriptive Notes Taken from the Scripture for Research

They Overcame Him

Revelation 12:11
And they overcame him by the blood of the Lamb, and by the word of their testimony; and they loved not their lives unto the death.

Hebrews 10:21-23
Let us draw near with a true heart in full assurance of faith, having our hearts sprinkled from an evil conscience, and our bodies washed with pure water.

No Condemnation

Romans 8:1-8
There is now no condemnation to them which are in Christ Jesus. To be carnally minded is death; but to be spiritually minded is life and peace.

Romans 8:14-15
For as many as are led by the Spirit of God, they are the sons of God.

Believe and Speak the Word Only

Luke 8:49-55
Thy daughter is dead; trouble not the Master. But when Jesus heard it, he answered him, saying, Fear not: believe only, and she shall be made whole.

Matthew 8:7-10

And Jesus said to him, I will come and heal him. The centurion answered and said, Speak the word only, and my servant shall be healed.

Living in Two Realms

John 3:12-13

How shall you believe, if I tell you of heavenly things? And no man hath ascended up to heaven, but he that came down from heaven, even the Son of man which is in heaven.

Power Flowing

Habakkuk 3:4

And his brightness was as the light; he had horns coming out of his hand: and there was the hiding of his power.

Acts 5:12-16

They brought the sick into the streets, and laid them on beds and couches, that at the least the shadow of Peter passing by might overshadow some of them.

You are an Ambassador

II Corinthians 5:20

Now then we are ambassadors for Christ, as though God did beseech you by us: we pray you in Christ's stead, be you reconciled to God.

We Are Kings and Priests

Revelation 1:5-6
Jesus Christ, the prince of the kings of the earth, has made us kings and priests unto God and his Father.

Revelation 5:9-10
And has made us unto our God kings and priests: and we shall reign on the earth.

Your Body Is a Member of the Resurrected Christ

I Corinthians 6:15, 17
Know you not that your bodies are the members of Christ? But he that is joined unto the Lord is one spirit.

Colossians 2:9-15
For in him dwells all the fullness of the Godhead bodily. And you are complete in him, which is the head of all principality and power.

Colossians 1:14-18
And he is the head of the body, the church: who is the beginning, the firstborn from the dead; that in all things he might have the preeminence.

The Forty-Second Generation in Christ

I Peter 2:9
But you are a chosen generation, a royal priesthood, a holy nation, a peculiar people; that you should shew forth the praises of him who hath called you out of darkness into his marvelous light.

Matthew 1:17-18
All the generations from Abraham to David are fourteen generations; from David into Babylon are fourteen generations; from Babylon to Christ are fourteen generations.

I Thessalonians 5:4-6
Ye are all the children of light, and the children of the day: we are not of the night, nor of darkness.

Hebrews 7:15-28
He has an unchangeable priesthood. He is holy, harmless, undefiled, separate from sinners, and made higher than the heavens consecrated for evermore.

Hebrews 4:14-16
Let us therefore come boldly unto the throne of grace that we may obtain mercy, and find grace to help in time of need.

Deuteronomy 26:15-19
The LORD has affirmed you this day to be his peculiar people, to make you high above all nations, in praise, in name, and in honor; that you may be a holy people unto him.

I Peter 2:10
Which in time past were not a people, but are now the people of God: which had not obtained mercy, but now have obtained mercy.

I Corinthians 2:9-10
Eye has not seen, nor ear heard, neither have entered into the heart of man, the things God has prepared for them that love him. But God has revealed them to us by his Spirit.

The Lamb Slain to Receive

Revelation 5:11-14
Saying with a loud voice, 'Worthy is the Lamb that was slain to receive power, and riches, and wisdom, and strength, and honor, and glory, and blessing.'

Romans 8:16-17
And if children, then heirs; heirs of God, and joint-heirs with Christ; if so be that we suffer with him, that we may be also glorified together.

Receive Power

Matthew 28:18
And Jesus came and spoke unto them, saying, 'All power is given unto me in heaven and in earth.'

Receive and Give Wealth and Riches

I Timothy 6:17-19
Charge the rich not to be high-minded, but trust in the living God, who gives us richly all things to enjoy. Be rich in good works, ready to distribute, and willing to give.

Matthew 26:52-54
Do you think you that I cannot now pray to my Father, and he will immediately provide me with more than twelve legions of angels?

Receive and Release by Wisdom

Romans 1:19-20
For the invisible things of him from the creation of the world are clearly seen, being understood by the things that are made, even his eternal power and Godhead.

I Corinthians 1:20-22
Where is the wise? After that in the wisdom of God the world by wisdom knew not God, it pleased God by the foolishness of preaching to save them that believe.

II Timothy 3:14-17
All scripture is given by inspiration of God, and is profitable for doctrine, reproof, correction, and instruction in righteousness.

I Corinthians 2:4-5
My speech and my preaching was in demonstration of the Spirit and of power: that your faith should not stand in the wisdom of men, but in the power of God.

Proverbs 4:5-10
Wisdom is the principal thing; therefore get wisdom: and with all your getting get understanding.

Receive and Release Strength

Micah 5:4
He shall stand and feed in the strength of the LORD, in the majesty of the name of the LORD his God; and they shall abide.

Nehemiah 8:10
For the joy of the Lord is your strength.

Psalm 21:1
The king shall joy in your strength, O Lord; and in your salvation how greatly shall he rejoice!

Colossians 1:11
Strengthened with all might, according to his glorious power, unto all patience and longsuffering with joyfulness.

II Timothy 4:17
Notwithstanding the Lord stood with me, and strengthened me; that by me the preaching might be fully known.

Hebrews 9:16-17
For a testament is of force after men are dead: otherwise it is of no strength at all while the testator lives.

Receive and Give Honor and Glory

Hebrews 2:6-10
Jesus was made a little lower than the angels for the suffering of death, crowned with glory and honor; that he by the grace of God should taste death for every man.

I Peter 1 5-7
The trial of your faith, though it be tried with fire, might be found unto praise, honor, and glory at the appearing of Jesus Christ.

I Peter 5:10
The God of grace, who has called us unto his eternal glory by Christ Jesus, make you perfect, stablish, strengthen, and settle you. To him be glory and dominion forever.

Hebrews 1:3
Jesus Christ is the brightness of God's glory, and the express image of his person. Upholding all things by the word of his power, he sat down on the right of the Majesty on high.

Jude 1:24-25
God is able to present you faultless before the presence of his glory with exceeding joy. To the only wise God our Savior, be glory and majesty, dominion and power, forever.

Psalm 29:1-2
Give unto the LORD, O you mighty, give unto the LORD glory and strength. Give unto the LORD the glory due unto his name; worship the LORD in the beauty of holiness.

Receive Blessing and Bless

Psalm 21:13
Be thou exalted, LORD, in thine own strength: so will we sing and praise your power.

Psalm 96:1-3
O sing unto the LORD a new song: sing unto the LORD, all the earth. Sing unto the LORD, bless his name; shew forth his salvation from day to day.

Isaiah 42:9-11
Sing unto the LORD a new song, and his praise from the end of the earth, you that go down to the sea, and all that is therein; the isles, and the inhabitants thereof.

Psalm 145:1-21
I will bless and praise your name forever. Great is the LORD and greatly to be praised.

Revelation 5:9
You were slain, and has redeemed us to God by your blood out of every kindred, and tongue, and people, and nation.

Hebrews 2:11-12
For both he that sanctifies and they who are sanctified are all of one. He says, I will declare your name to my brethren, in the midst of the church will I sing praise unto you.

I Peter 1:8-9
Jesus, whom having not seen, you love; in whom, though now you see him not, yet believing, you rejoice with joy unspeakable and full of glory.

Colossians 3:16
Let the word of Christ dwell in you richly in all wisdom. Teach and admonish one another in psalms, hymns and spiritual songs; sing with grace in your hearts to the Lord.

Ephesians 5:18-20
Be filled with the Spirit, speaking to yourselves in psalms and hymns and spiritual songs, singing and making melody in your heart to the Lord. Give thanks.

Prosperity, Rest, Restoration, and Truth

Psalm 23:1-3
The LORD is my shepherd. I shall not lack. He makes me to lie down in green pastures, leads me beside the still waters, and restores my soul.

Matthew 6:33
But seek you first the kingdom of God, and his righteousness; and all these things shall be added unto you.

Matthew 13:18-23

But he that received seed into the good ground is he that hears the word, understands it, bears fruit, and brings forth.

Maintain Growth in Your Environment and Surroundings

Isaiah 55:10-13

So shall my word be that goes forth out of my mouth: it shall not return to me void, but it shall accomplish that which I please, and it shall prosper in the thing whereto I sent it.

Isaiah 61:10-11

For as the earth brings forth her bud, and as the garden causes the things that are sown in it to spring forth; so the Lord God will cause righteousness and praise to spring forth.

III John 1:2-4

Beloved, I wish above all things that you may prosper and be in health, even as your soul prospers. I have no greater joy than to ear that my children walk in the truth.

Greater Works

John 14:12-13

Greater works than these shall he do; because I go unto my Father. And whatsoever you shall ask in my name, that will I do, that the Father may be glorified in the Son.

CHAPTER 12

Living Life on the Other Side of Resurrection

The Preeminence of the Lord Jesus Christ

Early in the morning, the Holy Spirit is ready to move. Gem, now knowing how to maintain and grow his spiritual strength and power in the earth realm, is expecting his first assignment. "Gem," gently waking him, the Holy Spirit displays a black and white panoramic vision that progresses into brilliant color. Watching the film clip like vision, he suddenly realizes the Holy is showing him a view of his transformation from the helpless dirty puppet into the Lord's Worship Warrior Ambassador he is today.

Gem knows that whatever the Holy Spirit tells him to do, he is up to the challenge. He asks, "Holy Spirit, what are we doing today?" Before continuing, the Holy Spirit reminds him, "The miraculous realm of heaven on earth is in you. Your on-going faith assignment, living life on the other side of resurrection, is to discern and release the judgment and justice of the government of God everywhere you go and in everything you do. In righteousness, compassion, and grace, defend and meet the needs of those who have unknowingly allowed the kingdoms in the world system to control them. You know the life, love, and light of the Father, but many, many people have never experienced his goodness."

Gratefully Gem, responds, "You've made me strong enough to rest in my Father. I know, with you, I can see unlimited possibilities for others, and with wisdom and understanding, I can help them make the right choices. I am so grateful to my Father, to Jesus Christ, and you, Holy Spirit, for helping me see the light in freedom. The light of the knowledge of God will shine in their hearts when they hear and receive the gospel of Jesus Christ. Then when eternal light surrounds them, and they feel the love, they will know that you have translated them into his kingdom of eternal life and have delivered them from the darkness that separated you from them, Father. As you have helped me, I can help them hear God's voice, believe and experience hope, see unlimited possibilities in the light of his glory, and follow him. Thank you for showing me how to maneuver with infinite possibilities in the freedom of your glorious light!"

With words of assurance and preeminent victory, the Holy Spirit sends Gem into the world system equipped and ready, "God forever remains the same. All-powerful and all-knowing, he is present everywhere. Therefore, reveal the knowledge of God's glory to all people. Preach salvation through Jesus Christ and the resurrection from the dead. The Lord works with you, confirming the Word with miracles, signs, deliverance, and healings. At the sound of his name, every knee bows in heaven, in the earth, and under the earth. As you go, see the world's kingdoms become the kingdoms of our Lord and his Christ."

No matter what part of the world, the enemy's kingdoms operate in, since the resurrection, they belong to God. The devil runs the world system on the lowest levels of death, hate, and darkness, disregarding or controlling the needs of the people who live in them. Instead of allowing people to develop freely and progress in his kingdoms, he uses condemnation, fear, and stress against them strategically, manipulating and applying among other things, competition, jealousy, greed, and the controlling force of lack.

The kingdom of heaven, offering eternal life, love, and light with unlimited possibilities, provides governmental authority and dominion by faith to change and bring increase to people's lives. Deception, encouraged within the kingdoms of the world system, causes spiritual blindness resulting in unbelief and limited thinking. Deliverance and restoration are available to all whose lives are stagnated and controlled by mental and emotional strongholds built, fortified, and reinforced with negativity. These deeply planted seeds of negative beliefs cause people to produce, strengthen and send thoughts, emotions, and words that attack themselves and others under their influence with all kinds of sickness, disease, and programmed failure. Jesus Christ preached deliverance on mental and spiritual levels to the powerless and spiritually blind so they could see the light of the gospel and choose for themselves who to follow. To reach them on a physical level, he taught and healed them by demonstrating the power of his spoken Word.

Maintain your heavenly atmosphere, environment, surroundings, and anointing daily with gratitude and thanksgiving. Meditate with the Holy Spirit, listening and asking questions. Study the Word, pray in tongues, and live by the Spirit. See yourself engaging in what he has shown you. Change your thinking, how you see yourself, and your words. Be who he says you are now.

Always remain in a pliable position with the Holy Spirit. When you encounter a challenging situation or one that reminds you of your past, don't try to do things your way. The Holy Spirit knows the truth about you and every person you encounter. Do not frustrate the grace of God with your idea of righteousness. Do not fall prey to your emotions, good or bad. Pause, listen for his voice, or look to see what he shows you. Then, with love and compassion, say what he says, or do what he shows you. If you don't hear or see anything in the spirit, wait until you do. Don't make something up out of emotion or embarrassment because you are trying to be their answer. Always allow God to work through you in wisdom and power.

The law of the Spirit of life in Christ Jesus makes people free from the law of sin and death that runs the world. Being drawn into the way of eternal life by the Spirit of God invites people to leave the control of the enemy and come to God through Christ Jesus. He is the way, the truth, and the life for them. Only by him can they come to the Father, receive the kingdom of heaven within, and all God is. Remain transparent with the Holy Spirit so he can use you as a spiritual weapon to turn their hearts towards God. He knows you inside and out. With God, there are no surprises. Praying in tongues allows him to work with you through any concerns you may have before you encounter the assignments of the day. Praying in tongues also clears, sharpens, and energizes your spirit and soul to work together with him and the angels in power and love.

People who disregard or have not experienced the goodness and power of God seek to be in control of themselves with something or someone they can see and touch. They sometimes look to worship and obey or receive wisdom and power from other people or manmade things, such as images or statues. To replace God's authority over their lives with another person or with something they have made is to say, 'Me, Myself, and I' will be in charge of my life. Turning their backs to God is rejecting his goodness, all he is, and the protection of his right hand. By refusing eternal life through Jesus Christ, their one possibility of freedom, they remain under the law of sin and death.

He has provided peace. By faith and grace, without condemnation, he opened the way through the veil to the throne of God's mercy. Jesus proclaimed the fulfillment of the acceptable year of the Lord before he began his ministry and from the cross at his crucifixion, declaring, "It is finished." Initiating the New

Covenant in his Blood, he said, "Father, into your hands, I commend my spirit." He bowed his head and gave up his spirit. He then descended into the lowest parts of the earth into hell, suffered for you, stripped principalities and powers from the enemy, preached to the spirits in prison, and then led the captives to heaven with him. Jesus Christ finished his ministry and life on earth victoriously.

The day of the vengeance of our God, as stated in Isaiah chapter 61, verse 2, has been now, since the resurrection of Jesus Christ. Jesus Christ preached and fulfilled the acceptable year of the Lord, and now is the day of vengeance of our God. The vengeance of God began with the resurrection of Jesus Christ. He did not mince his words from the cross when he said, "It is finished." He had announced to those who were plotting to kill him, "Destroy this temple, and in three days, I will raise it up." His resurrection by the power of God sent a clear message to all who would receive it. All people are potentially saved and have the opportunity to experience the benefits of salvation now. Instituting kingdom judgment and justice from God's throne establishes restoration and restitution for all.

After restoring God's relationship and complete provision for humanity, Jesus Christ then addressed the church. He commanded them to wait for the power of the Holy Spirit and do even greater works for God in his name. The bold message he delivered to all is that the gates of hell cannot prevail against the church. They have the keys of the kingdom of heaven with instructions to use them. The Lord's vengeance is against the devil and not people. It is a spiritual battle that Jesus has already won. You are to speak and preach, demonstrating the Spirit and power of God's wisdom, so their faith stands in the power of God and not in the wisdom of men. Preaching the good news of the gospel by the wisdom of God does not condemn or destroy people. Preach it to draw them to God through Jesus Christ. He came to destroy the works of the devil, not people.

To comfort all that mourn, God begins with the individual as he did with Abraham, John the Baptist, and Jesus Christ.

Today, he starts with you. He provided everything you will ever need to be successful in life and ministry before you were born. God called you alone; to receive salvation is a personal decision. To fulfill your calling from God is also a personal decision, but includes help from him. It doesn't matter if you are male or female, your ethnicity, or your circumstance, you are one in Christ Jesus with all those who by faith have made him their Lord. You are the building, the temple of the Holy Spirit, built upon the foundation of the apostles and prophets, Jesus Christ himself is the chief cornerstone. You are not only a fellow citizen with all the saints of the household of God but a king, a priest, and an ambassador unto God. In Jesus Christ, you are part of the building that is fitly framed together and growing into a holy habitation of God through the Spirit. Yes, the temple of the Holy Spirit in the Lord, where God abides, is in the kingdom of God within you. Here, your relationship, in the presence of God, the Lord Jesus Christ, and the Holy Spirit, grows stronger in power, spirit, wisdom, and grace. Your relationship with the Godhead translates into everyone you meet, all you do, and everywhere you go.

The Holy Spirit directs you to people under the pressures of the world who he has designated for you to help. Exercising your right to operate in two realms simultaneously, listen and look to the Holy Spirit while talking to them. Be sensitive to what you see or hear about them and use wisdom. Set their spiritual appointment for them to receive beauty for ashes, the oil of joy for mourning, and the garment of praise for the spirit of heaviness. Begin by seeing the celebration of joy on the person's face in your imagination because, according to the finished work of Jesus Christ, they now have what they desire. Understanding and knowing this, speak to the problem from faith in your heart in the name of Jesus. Do not allow any contrary thoughts to enter your mind. By exercising this discipline, you allow 100% of the power needed from God to flow through you at that moment from the heavenly realm into them. Give God the praise and glory.

Giving God praise when he uses you to turn a situation around for yourself or someone else opens the door for a conversation about salvation. When the goodness and power of God are on display, the finished work of Jesus cannot be denied. Teaching them how to believe for what they see, and then by faith release the power of God in Jesus' name, turns everything around for them. Since God created everything good, his will for them is to receive his goodness. His message to them is to believe he has already provided what they need to reverse their lives from experiencing evil to good. Negative words and emotions block the truth and build mental strongholds that resist and prevent the increase of their capacity to believe for the limitless possibilities that are available for them to achieve.

In the world system, the three temptations of the devil in operation are still the lust of the eyes, the flesh, and the pride of life. Teaching and demonstrating the kingdom, power, and glory of God turns the attention of the people to him. God's command to not eat or learn from the tree of knowledge of good and evil is still in effect. To turn their lives around through the preaching of the gospel, God offers himself to all by telling them to choose life and blessing. He is their life and the length of their days. They cannot serve God and serve the devil at the same time. People should understand that God is pure light. He will not change himself for anyone because his mighty power and glory that flows from his throne to the earth, not vice versa.

In the kingdoms of the world system are people whose spiritual ears and eyes need to open to the endless love and power of God. The enemy's influence is present and active in the realms that have not submitted to God's ruling government. These areas in the kingdoms of the world, with multiple levels associated with them, are family, religion, education, finance, government, media, and arts and entertainment. God's original command to humanity was to be fruitful, multiply, replenish the earth, subdue it and have dominion in every part of these areas and more have not changed. The name of Jesus is above any other name. With the preeminence of the Lord Jesus Christ mindset that says every knee must bow to the sound of his name, vengeance, and restoration with restitution from the enemy is imminent.

Individual people make up the world's population. God began his relationship with humanity, male and female before he created and made them in his image and after his likeness. Speaking the Word by the Spirit, he filled the earth and the heavens with the light of his presence. For them, he became all the provision, support, guidance, and intelligence they would ever need to grow up spiritually, learning to imitate him. All was good, and all things were possible for them to have, create, multiply, etcetera. He was their loving Father. God made individuals to live forever. They were to manifest his will across the earth and possibly the heavens by the knowledge of his glory. We move spiritually by the vengeance of the Lord to lift them above the crowd and turn them 180 degrees to a new spiritual perspective and perception.

Multitudes of people from various nations, cultures, languages fill the earth. Each culture, in different forms, support the areas of family, religion, education, economics, government, media, and arts and entertainment. Although people form, establish, or build and in some capacity control, each area, the existing problems are not caused by people, but by the enemy who influences them. Therefore, whether they are aware of it or not, he controls the people, their success or failures, and their areas of power and influence in the various regions in his kingdoms. Because of the negative thought power and influence of the world system, no nation is without its problems. Their progress, issues, and levels of suffering vary, but the pain is real none the less. The answers to all the setbacks, anxiety, and distress exist. It lies in each person and no one else.

Their answer begins with awareness and then the eye-opening realization that they can live a life of freedom from the spiritual realm where they are right now. The demonstration of the Word of God and power, no matter how small, will build assurance of God's willingness to assist them and lead them to make changes in their daily lives. The arm of God is not short concerning those who call upon him in times of trouble. He is ready to show himself strong to all those who call upon him. He is ready to restore them to himself. Using their will, they can overcome the negative familiarity that keeps them in bondage and make a firm decision to obtain their freedom. Once they take this step of freedom, their transformation begins within. The Spirit of God leads them to position their thinking, imaginations, words, and their lives to overcome with the power of preeminence in the name Jesus.

God desires to reach all peoples in the world system with the restoring power of his love. Whether they are male or female, bond or free does not matter to him. They are his family, and his desire is for people to return to him. His government brings people judgment and justice, which is good. God desires a relationship, not religion. Education for all is from the limitless knowledge of the Holy Spirit. They become a member of the chosen generation media that speaks blessings into the lives of people. Because they speak blessings and not negativity, they prosper materially and become or remain healthy. The answer is in them. God put eternity in their hearts, and the way to eternity with the one who made them is salvation through the Lord Jesus Christ.

The world and the fullness thereof belongs to God. The heaven, even the heavens, are the LORD's, but the earth has he given to the children of men. How is this possible? You are his child. Some may not realize that they are potentially his, but that is your assignment. Live unto your Lord and Savior Jesus Christ, gratefully following his commands. With authority, use his position of preeminence, the power of his Blood, and his name. Discern, defend, and meet the needs of the people in righteousness, compassion, and grace. By faith, release his resurrection power. See it flow out of you into them. With the help of the Holy Spirit and the angels, face-off the enemy in how you think, what you see, imagine, say and do in his name. Know that the preeminence of the Lord Jesus Christ always gives you victory.

The miraculous realm of heaven on earth is in you. Living life on the other side of resurrection in the kingdom of Jesus Christ is full of power and excitement. Protect your atmosphere, environment, surroundings, and anointing in the anointed Jesus. To see and experience changes in peoples' lives no matter who they are, what they have experienced, good or bad, or where they live is life-changing. By the power of God, open and shut doors in the name of Jesus. Do not settle for what others call normal. Follow the Holy Spirit and the Word of life. Keep your heart with all diligence. Life flows out of it. Believe and speak God's will from your heart, for with God, all things are possible.

PART 5: THE KINGDOM LIFESTYLE

Chapter 12

Summary Questions
&
Reference Scriptures

PART 5: THE KINGDOM LIFESTYLE
Chapter 12 Summary Questions

Living Life on the Other Side of Resurrection
The Preeminence of the Lord Jesus Christ

1. Why is it essential to define and rehearse your position in Jesus Christ before moving out in your daily assignment?

2. What is the difference between the enemy's world system, his kingdoms, and the areas of his operation?

3. Why should you maintain and protect your anointing?

4. What should you do when you encounter a difficult situation?

5. How do you remain transparent so the Holy Spirit can use you as a spiritual weapon?

6. What was Jesus referring to when he said, "It is finished," from the cross?

7. Why is the day of vengeance of our God so important?

8. Do you understand why all peoples of the earth are so important to God?

9. On assignment, how do you obtain victory before you begin?

10. Knowing that with God, all things are possible, what is your part in bringing forth what you have planted in your heart to fruition?

Chapter 12 Scripture References
Descriptive Notes Taken from the Scripture for Research

Defend, Do Justice, Deliver

Psalm 82:1-8
How long will you judge unjustly, and accept the persons of the wicked? Defend the poor and fatherless: do justice to the afflicted and needy. Deliver the poor and needy.

The Kingdoms of This World

Matthew 4:8
Again, the devil takes him up into an exceeding high mountain, and shows him all the kingdoms of the world, and the glory of them.

Revelation 11:15
The kingdoms of this world are become the kingdoms of our Lord, and of his Christ; and he shall reign for ever and ever.

Revelation 7:9-10
A great multitude, which no man could number, of all nations, and kindred, and people, and tongues, stood before the throne, and before the Lamb, clothed with white robes.

God Shines in Their Hearts

II Corinthians 4:5-7
We preach not ourselves, but Christ Jesus the Lord. God has shined in our hearts, to give the light of the knowledge of the glory of God in the face of Jesus Christ.

Knowledge of the Glory

Habakkuk 2:14
For the earth shall be filled with the knowledge of the glory of the LORD, as the waters cover the sea.

Preach the Resurrection

Acts 4:2
Being grieved that they taught the people, and preached through Jesus the resurrection from the dead.

Every Knee Bows

Philippians 2:9-11
Wherefore God also hath highly exalted him, and given him a name which is above every name: That at the name of Jesus every knee should bow.

Mark 16:20
And they went forth, and preached everywhere, the Lord working with them, and confirming the word with signs following. Amen.

Compassion

Jude 1:20-25
And of some have compassion, making a difference. And others save with fear, pulling them out of the fire; hating even the garment spotted by the flesh.

II Corinthians 4:3-4
In whom the god of this world has blinded the minds of them which believe not, unless the light of the glorious gospel of Christ, who is the image of God, should shine unto them.

Do Not Frustrate Grace

Galatians 2:20-21
I live by the faith of the Son of God. I do not frustrate the grace of God: for if righteousness come by the law, then Christ is dead in vain.

No Condemnation

Romans 8:1-2
There is no condemnation to those in Christ Jesus who walk after the Spirit. The law of the Spirit of life in Christ Jesus has made me free from the law of sin and death.

John 14:6
Jesus said unto him, I am the way, the truth, and the life: no man comes to the Father, but by me.

Man's Wisdom, Authority, and Images

Genesis 3:5-7
When the woman saw that it was a tree to be desired to make one wise, she took of the fruit thereof, and did eat, and gave to her husband with her; and he did eat.

I Samuel 8:1-22
Listen to the voice of the people in all that they say unto you: for they have not rejected you, but they have rejected me, that I should not reign over them.

Romans 1:20-25
Professing themselves to be wise, they became fools, and changed the glory of the incorruptible God into an image made like to corruptible man, and four-footed beasts.

Acts 17:28-31
Forasmuch then as we are the offspring of God, we ought not to think that the Godhead is like unto gold, or silver, or stone, graven by art and man's device.

Ephesians 5:9-17
See then that you walk circumspectly, not as fools, but as wise, redeeming the time, because the days are evil, understanding what the will of the Lord is.

Freedom

John 8:32
And you shall know the truth, and the truth shall make you free.

By Faith and Grace

Romans 4:16
Therefore it is of faith that it might be by grace; to the end the promise might be sure to all the seed.

It Is Finished

John 19:30
When Jesus therefore had received the vinegar, he said, "It is finished." He bowed his head, and gave up the ghost.

Luke 23:46
And when Jesus had cried with a loud voice, he said, "Father, into your hands I commend my spirit." Having said thus, he gave up the ghost.

I Peter 3:18-19
For Christ also hath once suffered for sins, the just for the unjust, that he might bring us to God, being put to death in the flesh, but quickened by the Spirit. By which also he went and preached unto the spirits in prison.

Ephesians 4:8-10
Wherefore he said, when he ascended up on high, he led captivity captive. He also descended first into the lower parts of the earth that he might fill all things.

The Day of Vengeance

Isaiah 61:2
To proclaim the acceptable year of the LORD, and the day of vengeance of our God; to comfort all that mourn.

John 2:19
Jesus answered and said unto them, "Destroy this temple, and in three days I will raise it up."

Isaiah 9:7

Upon the throne of David, and his kingdom, to order it, and establish it with judgment and justice from henceforth even forever. The zeal of the LORD hosts will perform this.

The Gates of Hell

Matthew 16:18-19

Upon this rock I will build my church; and the gates of hell shall not prevail against it. And I will give unto you the keys of the kingdom of heaven.

Speak and Preach with God's Wisdom

I Corinthians 2:1-10

My speech and preaching was not with enticing words of man's wisdom, but in demonstration of the Spirit and power, that your faith should stand in the power of God.

Jesus Destroyed the Works of the Devil

I John 3:8

He that commits sin is of the devil; for the devil sins from the beginning. For this purpose the Son of God was manifested, that he might destroy the works of the devil.

He Called You Alone

Isaiah 51:1-2

Look unto Abraham your father, and unto Sarah that bare you: for I called him alone, and blessed him, and increased him.

Galatians 3:26-28
There is neither Jew nor Greek, there is neither bond nor free, there is neither male nor female: for you are all one in Christ Jesus.

Ephesians 2:19-22
You are built upon the foundation of the apostles and prophets, Jesus Christ himself being the chief corner stone in whom all the building is fitly framed together.

Luke 17:21
Neither shall they say, Lo here! or, lo there! for, behold, the kingdom of God is within you.

Minister Directed by the Holy Spirit

Ephesians 3:7
Whereof I was made a minister, according to the gift of the grace of God given unto me by the effectual working of his power.

Habakkuk 3:4
And his brightness was as the light; he had horns coming out of his hand: and there was the hiding of his power.

Philippians 4:19
But my God shall supply all your need according to his riches in glory by Christ Jesus.

The Knowledge of Good and Evil

Genesis 2:16-17
And the LORD God commanded the man, saying, "Of every tree of the garden you may freely eat: But of the tree of the knowledge of good and evil, you shall not eat of it."

Choose Life

Deuteronomy 30:14-20
I call heaven and earth to record this day against you, that I have set before you life and death, blessing and cursing: therefore choose life that both thou and your seed may live.

Matthew 6:24-34
No man can serve two masters. Either he will hate the one, and love the other; or else he will hold to the one, and despise the other. You cannot serve God and mammon.

Call in in the Day of Trouble

Psalm 50:15
And call upon me in the day of trouble: I will deliver you, and you shall glorify me.

Isaiah 59:1
Behold, the LORD's hand is not shortened, that it cannot save; neither his ear heavy, that it cannot hear.

II Chronicles 16:9
For the eyes of the LORD run to and fro throughout the whole earth, to show himself strong in the behalf of them whose heart is perfect toward him.

The Fullness of the Earth is the Lord's

Psalm 24:1
The earth is the LORD's, and the fullness thereof; the world, and they that dwell therein.

Psalm 115:15-16

You are blessed of the LORD which made heaven and earth. The heaven, even the heavens, are the LORD's: but the earth has he given to the children of men.

Preeminence

Colossians 1:17-18

He is before all things. By him all things consist. He is the head of the body, the church. He is the beginning, the firstborn from the dead. In all things he has the preeminence.

ACKNOWLEDGEMENTS

I send my appreciation and thanks to my husband, children, and grandchildren, who always encourage and support me as I follow the will of God for my life. In the kingdom, the power and glory of my Father God, the Lord Jesus Christ, and the Holy Spirit, I can hear, see, and do all things.

ABOUT THE AUTHOR

Hila J. Esters is an author, teacher, speaker, and consultant who helps people awaken to their unique God-given potential, enabling them to cut the strings of the status-quo, step into unlimited possibilities, and change their lives. Freedom is the real option. Hila is the founder of My Realm Live, which serves people who refuse to settle because they know life holds more for them.

From the age of three, Hila has had continual conversations with God. Throughout her life, no matter what situations, setbacks, or emotional heartbreaks she has faced, receiving and applying his revelation, wisdom, and knowledge has never failed. She especially enjoys his presence and is used by the Holy Spirit to 'freely receive and freely give.' Hila is the mother of two lovely daughters and is blessed to have four grandchildren. God's gift to Hila is her husband, Martin, who is truly from the heart of God.

ABOUT MY REALM LIVE

My Realm Live
The Kingdom Lifestyle

with
Hila J. Esters
MyRealmLive.com

TRANSFORM YOUR POWER.
STRATEGIZE YOUR POSITION.
EXPERIENCE THE FREEDOM.

Freedom is the real option. Moving with the crowd will only take you where the crowd is going. Discover your pivotal key moment and opportunity for change. Use it to break free! Rise above what they see, how they think, and what they say and do. In the silence you can hear, then see new possibilities for your life. The Kingdom Lifestyle – it's your choice. For more information go to – MyRealmLive.com.

YOUR NEXT STEPS WITH

The Miraculous Realm of Heaven on Earth
Living Life on the Other Side of Resurrection

☑ **TAKE THE FREE ASSESSMENT:**
Discover your Pivotal Key Moment and Opportunity for Change

☑ **EXPERIENCE HILA'S FREE MASTERCLASS:**
Cut the Strings and Step into Unlimited Possibilities

☑ **DO THE MIRACULOUS REALM BOOTCAMP**
Develop My Realm Live in Your Life

☑ **JOIN THE MASTERMIND:**
Become an Ambassador for the Lord Jesus Christ with Immunity

TheMiraculousRealm.com

No matter where you are in life, who you have become, or what you have done, God sees you as he originally made you - in his image. **Daddy's Little Girl,** the story of Hila's life from the age of three, is for everyone.

Making her life God's business, sent Hila on a journey of miracles, signs, and wonders as she faced, experienced, and overcame adversity.

DaddysLittleGirlMiracles.com

Teach, heal, and deliver - with God, all things are possible. Follow the flow of the Holy Spirit from the Glory of God, through the Redeeming Blood of Jesus Christ, to Resurrection Glory.

Signs, wonders, and miracles follow as you go from faith to faith and glory to glory.

YourDaddysSoBig.com

Reflections of Real Life Ministries

RORLMedia YouTube Channel

Hila J. Esters is a prolific teacher, author, and minister of the Gospel of Jesus Christ. Hila ministers the Word in power! Her passion is to reach people, give them the choice of freedom in Christ, then teach them how to live in the NOW of eternal life from the glory of the heavenly realm.

Learn how to receive, believe, and speak the past tense of God's Word, thereby releasing the resurrection power of the Lord Jesus Christ to bring transformative change in your life and the lives of others.

Continue to experience *The Miraculous Realm of Heaven on Earth.* Live life on the other side of the resurrection of Jesus Christ!

Subscribe Today!